The Law of Attraction
How It Really Works...
Honest! ™

Set sail on the adventure of your
life and become the captain
of your destiny!

Tim Hoehn

SeaDog Press, LLC

Decatur, Indiana

2013

ISBN 978-0-9892751-0-1

The author of this book is not a medical doctor and
does not dispense medical advice of any sort or
prescribe the use of any specific technique as a form of
treatment for physical or medical problems without the
advice of a physician. The intent of the author is to offer
information of a general nature that he has garnered on
his own and has proven helpful to him in the hope that
it will also prove helpful to you. If you choose to use any
of the information in this book yourself, which is your
right, the author and publisher assume no
responsibility for your actions.

Dedication

To Mike Bonin, Karen Beals, and Don Mack
~ my friends ~

Thank you for persevering to teach me the principles of intentionality. It was through the genuine passion that I saw uniquely displayed in each of you, and that you collectively and lovingly instilled in me, that I went on to identify and pursue my true purpose in life - writing.

You gave me the courage to "create what I want" and for that I will be forever in your debt.

Acknowledgements

To SeaDog Press, my publisher, thank you for providing a platform for new authors to present their work to the world.

To the many authors and scientists of the past and present who have learned of this great law and have persevered through their writings and teachings to make sure it is preserved and propagated for future use, thank you for your enlightenment, passion, and labors.

To the many people who have shared their personal life experiences concerning this subject matter with me, thank you for opening your heart.

Finally, to my good friend Deborah Shenefield, I thank you for introducing me to this entire line of thinking, and for providing me with abundant resource material for my research. Your kindness is a testament to your true understanding of this entire philosophy.

About The Author

This is the first book I have written and I'm kind of getting to the party a little late in life I guess. As I write this, I am in my mid-sixties having just recently discovered the full reality of the great truth of the wonderful Law of Attraction.

This law, in its current popular usage, simply states that you attract into your life what you think about, and that applies to both good and bad. As a matter of fact, you have been using this law your entire life but probably have not been aware of it - most people aren't. While its origins are not in the bible, its concept is written about in Proverbs 23:7 (MKJV) which simply states:

"For as he thinks in his heart, so is he ..."

Due to my life's path, I have some unique perspectives about this law that will help anyone understand how and why it works. I first truly grasped its relevance just recently and am at the beginning of my personal journey to create the life I have truly wanted all these years. My attempts to invoke this law positively on my behalf have been very successful, and it is that success which propels me forward.

I will tell you right up front that I have a religious background with a bible college degree and I am also a mechanical engineer. I have not done any pastoral work for close to twenty years now, but spent twenty-five years in pastoral ministry immediately after graduating from college.

At the conclusion of my pastoral years, I actually gave up on organized religion, being very discouraged by what I perceived to be an institution that had lost its way. Sadly, almost as a proof of what I had observed, none of my colleagues with whom I had been very close friends for decades would even return my phone calls of continuing friendship. I was at a loss to explain to my children why their friends were now ignoring them.

But my spiritual life is so much richer today than it has ever been, and I feel more aligned with God and the universe than I ever have. I know that all of my past life experiences have been specifically orchestrated to bring me to this time because I have something very important to contribute.

When I thoroughly examined this law's premise and researched its presence in history, and more importantly to me, in scripture, I quickly recognized the all-too-familiar intelligence behind this law as the only source from which something so simple yet so powerful could have originated. God was at it again, surprising me, thrilling me, challenging me, and leading me into yet another totally new and exciting phase of my life.

I'm not going to do a lot of bible quoting in this work for it is not meant to be a spiritual book. But recently I read a verse that sums up my feeling about the presentation of these thoughts at this time.

Esther 4:14 (KJV) says
> "... and who knoweth whether thou
> art come to the kingdom for such a
> time as this?"

I guess the dichotomy of my career as an engineer and a devout student of the Bible and other spiritual writings has uniquely positioned me to be able to understand in great detail the spiritual side of this law along with the quantum mechanics side of the universe that works in harmonious concert with this law. These two things are inextricably and eternally intertwined and are awe-inspiring.

I feel like my life to this point has been like an orchestra ready to play a great concert; the tuning up in the pit has taken me more than sixty years, and now I am ready for the symphony to begin. If the tune-up and preparation has taken that long, how grand will the concert be?

One of the jobs I had in my engineering career was working at Fermilab in Batavia, IL. Named for the noted Italian physicist Enrico Fermi, Fermilab is, or was (they recently de-commissioned the particle accelerator), a proton accelerator and was the first super-conducting proton accelerator in the world. The main ring of the accelerator is buried in the ground just over forty miles west of downtown Chicago and is one mile in diameter. At the time I was there in the late 70's, it was operated by the US government's Department of Energy and still is today. Its stated purpose according to their official website is:

> "Scientists at Fermilab carry out research in high-energy physics to answer the questions: What is the universe made of? How does it work? Where did it come from?"[8]

The lab is located on the site of a ghost town which was named Weston, IL. At the time they moved in, there were numerous residential and commercial structures and an entire infrastructure in place. The existing houses and other buildings were converted to offices and other needed facilities. The Large Hadron Collider in Europe has now taken over as the center of collider experiments for the world of Particle Physics.

I was a member of the design team that created that super-conductor or the "super-conducting super-collider" as it was called. The team consisted of designers, engineers, scientists, physicists, chemists, and theorists, not to mention all of the administrators, electricians, plumbers, machinists, fabricators, clerical people, contractors, and lab technicians who put it all together and made it all work.

The new particle accelerator consisted of a main ring in which hundreds of twenty-two feet long dipole magnetic coils were located end to end in a circular design. Between each dipole coil was a small quadra-pole steering coil which provided the means of making the ring circular and steered the protons through a slight course change to again shoot straight down the next twenty-two foot section of dipole coil at very near the speed of light. All of this was housed within equally-sized cryostats which provided the means for the cryogenic super-cooling with multiple layers of insulation and circulating refrigerants. As might be expected, it required vast quantities of electrical energy to make it all work.

It was in actuality an amazing amalgam of science, theory, and human ingenuity; and in retrospect, a tribute to the Law of Attraction, the very law this book is written about. For as you will see as you read on, thoughts become things, and it was a series of thoughts that originally germinated in the mind of physicists and their belief in those thoughts that brought this lab into existence.

It was also very volatile at times. Hydrogen exists in its liquid state at -452F after extreme compression and can only be pumped through other components at a maximum of about three pounds per square inch (psi). Any more than that and it will begin to generate enough heat to make it pass from its liquid state to its gaseous state - called quench - and when that happens, unthinkably large amounts of energy are released almost instantaneously with potentially catastrophic results. We conducted several sector tests early-on when we would test a single twenty-two foot section for functionality. Several of the early tests saw helium quenches which almost completely destroyed large steel support structures. I've seen four 6" diameter threaded studs that were anchoring one end of the dipole cryostat bent over ninety degrees like they were drinking straws. That's why the sector tests were all conducted behind very thick sections of acrylic.

The original accelerator ring, located next to the new installation, was not able to produce the power required to go to places they wanted to go with research and exploration into the origins of the universe so the new super-conductor was created. As stated, it operated in temperatures produced by liquid helium at -452F, or very near absolute zero which is usually listed at -459.67F. At temperatures near absolute zero, electrical resistance is virtually nonexistent and thus more power can be generated.

As a benefit of my tenure at Fermilab, I have an insider's understanding of what smashing atoms is all about, and the thrill and excitement of peering into the world of quantum physics or as it also known, the microcosm. (I have another work on the way you might want to read entitled "The Big Bang Theory … What If …?". It addresses the subject matter of the quantum world in greater detail.)

On the spiritual side, I have been a student of the bible and other spiritual writings for more than forty years, and that is generally my default frame of reference. As you will see, it has given me some unique insights into the Law of Attraction. I never did just blindly swallow the "company line" and carved out my own set of beliefs about what the bible and other books did or did not teach. After all, if it didn't work for me as an individual,

I certainly couldn't teach it to others with any conviction.

One of the things I saw early on was that, contrary to what I read in the text books, there was a striking convergence between the tenets of scientific law and theory and the role of God in the universe. I didn't see the two as polar opposites at all as was being touted in the press and literature of the day. I guess I just didn't swallow anything that either was saying without verifying it for myself.

My introduction to this whole matter of the Law of Attraction came initially through listening to a set of CDs by Dr. Wayne Dyer on "The Power of Intention". A friend gave them to me and I approached them a bit skeptically due to my bible college training. I had been introduced to the philosophy of "intentionality" at my place of employment where they had invested in and adopted a leadership training program called Radical Leadership and Conscious Company to develop their employees.

At the heart of the program that was developed by Therese Kienast, the founder of Radical Leadership, was this teaching of being "intentional" about everything you do in life. They imparted to our company, by teaching and practical application, many specialized tools to assist us in being intentional, and I felt a strong kinship with the concepts they presented since they were closely aligned with my spiritual background. Dr. Dyer's CD set titled "The Secrets of the Power of Intention" piqued my curiosity and I decided to give them a listen while driving to work every day. After listening for just a couple of days, I also bought the book on which the CDs were based. I was so taken by what I heard and read that I have since bought several copies of the book and sent them to my friends with the hope that their lives will be as positively impacted as mine has been. In Dr. Dyer's book, which was written in 2004, one of the predictions he made is that intention would become the new buzz word for the next decade. As the decade has unfolded, his suspicions were very much on target.

After reading Dr. Dyer's book and listening to his CDs, I obtained a copy of the best-selling book "The Secret" by Rhonda Byrne. The entire volume of her book is devoted solely to the Law of Attraction. Reading it further piqued my interest in the specifics and implementation of this law and thus helped to propel this work. I have since purchased her audio CDs on "The Secret" and have listened to them more than one hundred times. Every time I listen I learn something new, something I didn't quite understand before and it has been very inspiring. She has come under a lot of criticism for her work but my personal evaluation is that she knows more about the Law of Attraction than anyone else I have read or come into contact with.

Since being acquainted with this topic by Dr. Dyer and Rhonda Byrne, I have spent hundreds of hours personally researching this subject and reading present day authors as well as many from the past including Charles Haanel, Robert Collier, Neville Goddard, U.S. Andersen, Andrew Carnegie, Napoleon Hill, William Clement Stone, Wallace Wattles, James Allen, Lynne McTaggart, and Dr. David Hawkins. My intention in writing this book is to bring you face-to-face with this law and expose you to its amazing power and simplicity. It is also my intention to fully explain how this law actually works, and thus provide you with real tools to successfully implement this law and predict reasonable expectations of its results in your life. My only request of you, the reader, is that you try to set aside pre-conceived notions about this law and approach it with an open mind and genuine, childlike, curiosity. I think you will be happy with your discoveries.

Contents

Introduction – Page 17

Chapter 1 – Page 22
The Law of Attraction: Fact or Fiction?

Chapter 2 – Page 45
The Law of Attraction:
How It Really Works ... Honest! ™

Chapter 3 – Page 65
Creating Proper Thoughts for the Law Of Attraction

Chapter 4 – Page 95
Preparing For the Harvest

Chapter 5 – Page 109
Obstacles in Your Way

Chapter 6 – Page 128
The Garden of the Universe

Chapter 7 – Page 161
The Language of Thought

Chapter 8 – Page 178
When Forbidden Fruit Becomes Food For Thought

Epilog – Page 203

Bibliography – Page 208

Introduction

The last several years have been filled with books, movies, blogs, essays, CDs, television shows, radio shows, seminars, and ... well you get the picture ... about the Law Of Attraction. And I guess rightfully so since it is an amazing phenomenon and has been there, mostly unobserved, since the universe began.

Just like every other law of the universe, the Law of Attraction is something you have been using since your life began, you probably just have not known about it. Before you knew anything about the law of gravity, you were aware of its daily effect in your life even if you didn't fully understand it or know its name. You perhaps observed its affects in action while playing sports as a child and seeing a ball fall to the ground with predictability.

Most of you probably don't have a deep understanding of the laws governing the transference, conservation, and movement of electrical energy but that doesn't hinder you from turning on a light switch as you enter a dark room. You may have never even heard of Daniel Bernoulli, a Swiss physicist who lived from 1700 to 1782, but you probably have no qualms about climbing aboard a commercial airliner and expecting it to safely fly you to your destination.

Bernoulli was the person who in 1738 published what is commonly known as Bernoulli's Principle which the Wright brothers adopted to construct their first Wright Flyer. Amazingly, observing birds in flight, helped lead to this law's discovery and the birds have been using this law forever and they certainly have no understanding of its existence or functionality as far as we know. Leonardo da Vinci, who lived from 1452 - 1519, was musing about human flight in his time by observing the flight characteristics of birds. And just as the Wright brothers and Leonardo da Vinci had their naysayers who swore there was no truth to the principles of flight, the Law of Attraction also has its detractors who totally discount, not only its premises, but also its very existence.

The universe is filled with laws that influence your daily life, many of them not even discovered yet, and you are probably only aware of a small handful of them. But when you do become aware of them, you gain a fuller understanding of their operation and are able to use them to your advantage. It is the same way with the Law of Attraction. You have been using it every day without knowing it and, due to that ignorance, have had no control over its results in your life. The concept of a universal law that works on your thoughts may seem very foreign; but thoughts are but one small portion of this law's area of influence.

So why has this ancient universal law of nature garnered so much attention recently? After all, it's been in existence for eons, so why now? Probably because of the ready access to power and wealth it portends to provide to all who will accept its simple tenets. Throughout recorded history, power and wealth have been the two most sought after achievements of a secular society. For centuries these deceitful twins have been the demarcation between the haves and the have-nots.

When I truly understood the claims of this law, my first question was can it really be that simple? I readily admit that the skeptic in me tended toward it being just another slick scam rather than a powerful member of nature's toolbox. My inquisitive nature demanded that I invest the time required to know the truth. How could I afford not to?

As I have studied this law from both a spiritual and scientific viewpoint I have been truly awed by its simplicity and yet it's promise of far-reaching ultimate power. What could be simpler than *you are what you think*? That's a very simple concept. And yet what could be more powerful and offer more promise and opportunity to mankind than *you are what you think*? The applications are limitless.

If true, and properly invoked, this law is potentially the obvious remedy to many of society's ills. It costs nothing monetarily to deploy and needs no further skills other than those present with us all at birth. Education is not needed, societal status is not needed, money is not needed, and even a basic understanding of the law is not needed. If the accounts are accurate all of us are already using this law and have been since birth, albeit not usually in our own best interest, and probably without realizing it. The major thing the supporters of this law say is needed is re-alignment, a mindset renewal, a course correction of sorts if you will.

You will soon read in Chapter 1 that many of this country's great business leaders in the past century were practitioners of the Law of Attraction. Men like Henry Ford, Thomas Edison, Andrew Carnegie, and John D. Rockefeller used this law to build their business empires.

But does the promise of this simple law also contain a darker side that could potentially summon all the evils of Pandora's Box? Can this law be used for evil as well as good? Now there is a question that must be definitively answered and there can be no equivocation on the answer, in my mind, if this law is to be recommended for use by all.

It is not my intention to be critical of other works on this subject. To the contrary it was these other works that served to whet my appetite and compel me to undertake this work. It is my intention, however, to disclose certain dimensions of understanding that I have not yet seen presented and thus heighten the understanding of all who purpose to make the Law of Attraction work with a positive impact on their behalf.

Chapter 1
The Law of Attraction: Fact or Fiction?

"A man is but the product of his thoughts, what he thinks, he becomes." - Ghandi

Is this whole Law of Attraction thing a scam - a way to get your money away from you?

Is it another one of those programs that promise the world but is impossible, due to its convolution of requirements, for the average person to implement?

Is it another one of those programs that sprinkles God's name and a few misquoted and misapplied Bible verses throughout the work to make you think it's spiritual and from God?

Is it just another "get-rich-quick" scheme?

So ... which is it ... fact or fiction?

I can imagine that many people reading this may be truly skeptical of the validity of the Law of Attraction. After all, how could anything reportedly that powerful really be that simple? C'mon!!! I understand your skepticism. I have been where you are.

This country in particular has been inundated with tricksters, scam artists, religious hucksters, and people who work the con game for years; all of whom are well dressed, look very successful, can cry crocodile tears on demand, speak eloquently and very convincingly, and have large TV advertising budgets. They come from every quarter of our global society promising the ability to have what you want, mostly unlimited wealth, if you just follow their simple, easy-to-understand, plan. They have slick marketing techniques and attractively packaged products, and they have very impressive looking resumes with reportedly impeccable credentials. But in the end, the experience of most patrons is that they commit some of their hard-earned money to buy into this plan and the only ones who are benefitted are the grifters who devised the plan.

In order to answer your skepticism, verify this law's existence, and fully understand it's mode of functionality, we need to lay some ground work about all of the universal laws of nature and how they work. Unfortunately, there continue to be unscrupulous people in the fringes of society and others looking to be opportunists whose only concern is the commercialization of this law and turning a quick profit from honest people desperate to secure a better life.

The Laws of the Universe

One thing my engineering background taught me was that there are hundreds of universal laws which govern the performance and functionality of our universe and they have been in existence since the universe began. The common understanding of a law is:

> "A scientific law or scientific principle is a concise verbal or mathematical statement of a relation that expresses a fundamental principle of science, like Newton's law of universal gravitation. *A scientific law must always apply under the same conditions, and implies a causal relationship between its elements* (emphasis mine).The law must be confirmed and broadly agreed upon through the process of inductive reasoning."[7]

As this statement makes clear, in order for any principle, hypothesis, or theory to be elevated to the status of a law, it must be "... confirmed and broadly agreed upon ..." In other words it must meet certain strict criteria, one of which is undeniable proof. That is one reason that Einstein's "Theory of Relativity" is still a theory and has never attained the status of a law - it has never been undeniably proven. Even though most modern scientists speak of Einstein's work as though it were law, many recent discoveries in Quantum Physics have seriously challenged the very core of his popular theory.

The true and actual physical laws of the universe must also work in harmony with each other and never conflict or contradict each other. Any other behavior would result in total chaos. That means that there will never be a physical law here on Earth that contradicts the law of gravity, and every other law must work in harmony with this law if they interface at all.

For example, the law of flotation depends on the law of gravity since the weight of the amount of water displaced by any boat is equal to the boat's weight. And as every elementary school student knows, weight is a product of the law of gravity. Weight and mass are not the same even though they are often times used interchangeably. As was demonstrated when our astronauts walked on the moon, whose gravity is about one-third that of the earth, the magnitude of the force of gravity affected how the astronauts were able to walk. On the moon, what would be on earth a standard stroll, turned out to be a bounding maneuver. Their mass was the same, but their weight on the moon was about one-third of that on earth and their muscles responded accordingly.

One of the greatest assets of the fact and nature of the laws that exist is that they also give absolute predictability to the outcome of their use. For example, NASA scientists and engineers depend on these laws and use them routinely to calculate the fuel required, the fuel burn rate, the velocity required, the insertion angle, and the planned trajectory for every mission that lifts off into space. That is how they so accurately land exploratory space craft on the Moon and Mars with exacting precision.

Ship builders around the world use the law of flotation to properly design and build the largest ships the world has ever seen, and appropriately distribute the load so that it controls in a predictable manner. Every time you step onboard an airliner, the pilots are required to perform a weight and balance calculation that assures that the center of gravity of the in-flight airplane will be within certain prescribed limits knowing that the law of gravity will treat any plane unkindly that lifts off outside of its center of gravity window.

The law of gravity is a very well-known universal law. Other examples of universal physical laws are the 1st, 2nd, and 3rd law of thermodynamics; Boyle's and Charles' law governing temperature, pressure, and volume; Ohm's law concerning electrical resistance; the law of the conservation of energy, etc. I will be focusing very shortly on a very basic, important, and pivotal universal law that will help you better understand the Law of Attraction.

Just as important, and arguably perhaps more important but lesser known to most people, are God's spiritual laws. And just like the physical laws of the universe, these spiritual laws all agree with each other and work in harmony with each other. These spiritual laws are not the Law of Moses which include what we commonly call the Ten Commandments. Those laws (actually 513 in number) were given to govern a nation. Some examples of a spiritual law are the law of faith, the law of spirit and life, etc.

Physical laws will never supersede spiritual laws; however, spiritual laws may at times be used to temporarily suspend physical laws when needed. And that really makes sense when you think about it since we know that the creator of the universe is in essence spirit and non-corporeal, and has created, or thought into being, all that we call matter or physical things from nothingness. The true essence and nature of who God is has the capacity to modify what he has created - it is the spirit that gives life!

The term most often used to describe the temporary suspension of a physical law is a miracle. Not all miracles are suspensions of physical laws, but all suspensions of physical laws are miracles, and I am using the term miracle in its strictest sense. Many people use the term *miracle of birth* for example; and while watching a human being born into this world is truly amazing, no physical laws have been suspended and Mother Nature is doing what she does every day. All of nature is truly awe-inspiring and a great tribute to the essence of the creative mind behind it all.

One other truth about these universal physical and spiritual laws that you need to know is that they don't require you to even know about them or believe them in order for them to work. You read that right - you don't have to even know or believe them for them to work - they are God's laws - not yours or mine, and they work whether or not you believe them. Sir Isaac Newton didn't publish his work on the law of gravity until 1687 but it has been working faithfully every second since the universe began. The tribal members of the most remote and isolated tribes in the world probably know nothing of the law of flotation yet they have been carving canoes out of trees and building rafts to cross rivers for centuries, all of which make use of the law of flotation.

These laws are also impersonal which means that they have no knowledge of who or what is making use of the law and possess no knowledge of good and bad, or right and wrong. A convicted murderer falling off of a tall building is no different than an innocent child falling off the same building to the law of gravity - they will both likely die in the fall.

In summarizing universal laws:

1. They have been in existence since the universe began pre-dating humanity
2. They work every time, no matter the circumstance
3. They work predictably the same every time
4. They are impersonal and work without knowledge of good and bad, or right and wrong
5. They cannot conflict or contradict any other law
6. Where they interface they must work in harmony with each other
7. They do not require knowledge of or belief in to work.

Much more could be written about universal laws and the manner in which they provide order and predictability to our universe, but with this basic knowledge of the functionality and behavior of universal laws, we are now ready to look at the Law of Attraction to determine - is it fact or fiction.

The Law of Attraction

History of This Law

In laying the ground work for a substantive evaluation of the validity of this law, it should be noted that the Law of Attraction and every other universal law pre-date humanity's arrival on the planet. They were not put into place with humanity specifically in mind. Who knows how long the universe existed before humans arrived. These laws could easily have been in place and functioning faithfully on other select targets in the universe for eons, and our planet earth is but one small speck in the vastness of our universe.

Whether you believe in creation, evolution or some other means of the universe getting here, the entire universe was here and complete before earth was populated with humanity. Accordingly then, we share equally with the rest of the universe in the functionality and promise of all of these laws.

Obviously then, the Law of Attraction was originally functioning and having an impact on things other than humanity's thoughts even though that seems to be the major focus of interest today. Early expressions of the Law of Attraction state it as **like attracts like**. The popular terminology of our current generation declares that **you attract back into your life the things that you think about,** which is actually a smaller subset and derivative of the original statement, since human thoughts are but one small, albeit very important, segment of this laws influence and use.

But this is only one manifestation of the unusual and quite extraordinary power of this law. I say unusual and extraordinary because the universal laws that most of us are acquainted with are very local in their reach and influence. For instance, Newton's law of universal gravitation only works on weak gravitational fields such as exist here on our planet and in our solar system. Ohm's law concerning electrical current, potential, and resistance only applies to linear networks. The Law of Attraction on the other hand, works throughout the entirety of our infinite universe. You can travel to the farthest reaches of our glorious celestial home - beyond the beyond - and there is no place that it is not faithfully functioning. If you happen to believe in alien life forms, this law works on their thoughts also! Perhaps ET should really consider phoning home!

So what else is governed by the Law of Attraction? Just as the law of gravity works on anything locally that possesses mass, the Law of Attraction has an equally impressive, although somewhat smaller client list also. Interestingly, gravity itself abides by the Law of Attraction at a very high level. Consider this statement.

> "Gravitation, or gravity, is a natural phenomenon by which physical bodies attract each other with a force proportional to their masses."[9]

So even though "physical body" is a very high level, nondescript, category, at that level "like attracts like" which by definition is the Law of Attraction.

A detailed study of Quantum Physics and Chemistry will yield a large inventory of things whose behavior is governed by and in compliance with the Law of Attraction. In Quantum Physics, for example, a subatomic particle called a Quark behaves according to this law. Consider the following statement:

"Quarks with unlike color charge attract one another as a result of the strong interaction, which is mediated by particles called gluons."[10]

Here we have a direct statement that certain Quarks attract each other and in the next section you will also read of other substances that behave in compliance with this law. Since this is not intended as a scientific manual, I will not belabor the point with detailed explanations of how it works with each. But now you know that this law is not the figment of some scammer's imagination who is waiting to pounce on your credit card. That is not to say that there are not scams using this law to bilk unwitting victims of their hard-earned money.

But knowing about this law and the specifics of its operational parameters will allow you to do what you desire most, completely control all the circumstances of your life. Your life will be what *you* decide it will be and no longer as you have been conditioned to believe just subject to the whims of chance - it's that simple. Let's briefly examine the origins and early recognition of this law in humanity.

Mentions of This Law in History

I thought it would be beneficial and add value to your learning experience to give you just a brief listing of some of the mentions of this law throughout human history. The first will be mentions in the Bible.

At the outset I said it was not my intention to be quoting bible verses often; this is one place that I will. I will only quote a couple which will establish a pattern, but there are hundreds more that could very easily be included.

While the Law of Attraction is not a spiritual law, the scriptures contain many references and allusions to it just as it does other universal laws.

For example, Acts 19:35 (KJV) relates

> "... and of the image which fell down from Jupiter"

An obvious reference to the influence of the law of gravity.

And another alluding to the force and effect of gravity in Acts 20:9 (KJV)

> "... and (he) fell down from the third loft, and was taken up dead".

The most-often quoted verse, and the one that very specifically states the reality and describes the functionality of the Law of Attraction, is Proverbs 23:7 (MKJV)

"For as he thinks in his heart, so is he".

That statement is very concise and needs no further explanation. It's as if God wanted to make sure that everyone who believes the bible is aware of this great law and realizes that its power is in its simplicity. If you believe that God said what He meant and meant what He said - this declaration needs no further clarification. As I used to tell people, "You don't need a four-year degree in theology to understand that"! There are no tricky or unusual words present that might be interpreted differently - just ten, very simple, single-syllable words, none of which is more than six letters long. It doesn't get much plainer or more direct than that.

Daniel 2:29 (KJV) reads:

> "As for thee, O king, thy **thoughts** came into thy mind upon thy bed, what should come to pass hereafter ..." (emphasis mine)

It is very apparent that Daniel is telling the king that the specific thoughts that he had while upon his bed would certainly be attracted back into his life and come to pass in just a short while. History records that is exactly what occurred.

Ephesians 3:20 (KJV) states

> "Now unto him that is able to do exceeding abundantly above all that we ask or **think,** according to the power that worketh in us". (emphasis mine)

In one of the most-often quoted verses in Christian circles, Paul is obviously telling the believers in Ephesus that God will bring back into their lives " ... exceeding abundantly above ... " whatever they think about and ask for. The natural progression is always to think about something before you ask for it so thinking is paramount in this verse.

And one last one – Philippians 4:8 (KJV) implores

> "Finally brethren, whatsoever things are true, whatsoever things are honorable, whatsoever things are just, whatsoever things are pure, whatsoever things are lovely, whatsoever things are of good

report; if there be any virtue, and if there be any praise, **THINK ON THESE THINGS**" (emphasis mine).

Paul gives an impressive list of eight things that he is instructing the believers in Philippi to think and concentrate on - Why Paul, why do you want them to think about those things? Because:

> "For as he thinks in his heart, so is he"
> Proverbs 23:7 (MKJV)

Paul knew that the quickest way for these believers to turn their lives around and become what God wanted them to be, was to think about and concentrate upon the right things, knowing all along that you attract back into your life what you think about. He had used this law successfully for years having been one of the most wicked despots and enemies of the early church.

His life had been literally transformed by this method and he clearly instructs the church at Rome in Romans 4:30 (KJV)

> "And be not conformed to this world, but be ye transformed by **the renewing of your mind,** that ye may prove what is

that good and acceptable, and perfect will of God". (emphasis mine)

Paul knew first-hand what he was talking about and desired to share that powerful practice with his brethren.

Somewhere between 490BC and 430BC, a Greek philosopher before the time of Socrates by the name of Empedocles put forth the thought of what he termed "attractive forces".

You may not know who Empedocles is, but just about everyone has heard of the great philosopher Plato. He is revered as one of the great thinkers of all time and in 391BC, inspired by the work of Empedocles, Plato postulated what he termed the first law of affinity as "likes tend toward likes". In other words - like attracts like. He had obviously observed something very important and cornerstone to his society which he was trying to describe and preserve for posterity sake. Plato had specifically observed and described attractions of earth to earth and water to water.

These laws of affinity were later known as the laws of attraction and included many different individual derivatives of the main theme produced by many different scientists.

Here are just a few notable ones.

"In 1250 Albertus Magnus applied the conception of 'affinity' to chemical systems and postulated four laws of affinity.

In 1687, Isaac Newton proposed that chemical affinities were due to certain forces that would likely follow similar laws analogous to the three laws of planetary motion. He expanded on these views in 'Query 31' of his 1704 Opticks.

In 1718, after translating Newton's Opticks, French physician and chemist Étienne Geoffroy proposed a new law of affinity that 'whenever two substances are united that have a disposition to combine and a third is added that has a greater affinity with one of them, these two will unite, and drive out the other.' Using this law, he published the first ever affinity tables.

In 1749, building on Geoffroy's affinity table, French chemist J. P. Macquer published six truths of chemical affinity, which encompassed both Plato's and Geoffroy's affinity laws, as well as four new ones. In 1766, he published seven types of affinity in his Dictionnaire de chymie.

With the discovery of sub-atomic particles, such as the quark (1964), and the fundamental forces, the term "laws of attraction" has been replaced with the conception of field particle exchange, and the bonding effect created therefrom. Subsequently, in the 20th century the laws of affinity were replaced by the laws of quantum chemistry and chemical thermodynamics."[2]

Leaders of Industry

The following is just a partial list of prominent 19th and 20th century devotees of the Law of Attraction. In his book "Think and Grow Rich", Napoleon Hill records that over a twenty year period, at the urging of Andrew Carnegie who was a devout believer and proponent of the Law of Attraction, he interviewed more than five hundred of the most prominent and influential people in the world, and each of them knew and practiced the

Law of Attraction. It reads like the "Who's Who" of industry, innovation, and business.

Henry Ford - founder of the Ford Motor Company and credited with the invention of the production line that so many businesses use today. The two men most prominent in developing Lean Manufacturing credit Henry Ford as their main source of inspiration. One of Ford's famous quotes alludes to the Law of Attraction:

> "If you think you can do a thing or think you can't do a thing, you're right."

William Wrigley Jr. - best known as the owner of Wrigley Chewing Gum he was also at one time the owner of Catalina Island off of the coast of Los Angeles. There he transformed the lazy island into a booming tourist attraction with the addition of a great infrastructure and commercial businesses. He also established the Pebble Beach quarry and tile plant to provide jobs for the local residents. He was also part-owner of the Chicago Cubs baseball team.

George Eastman - founder of the Eastman Kodak Company and inventor of many products we still use today. He was the first to create film on a roll which became the basis for the invention of motion picture film used in movies.

Andrew Carnegie - a Scottish-American industrialist, he worked his way up the ranks in industry and founded Carnegie Steel which became the pre-eminent steel company in the world. He led the expansion of the steel industry in the 19th century. Carnegie Steel through mergers and acquisitions became US Steel. He believed in giving back and built Carnegie Hall. He also founded Carnegie Mellon University, Carnegie Museums in Pittsburgh, Carnegie Institution in Washington, and the Carnegie Endowment for International Peace.

Thomas Edison - one of the most prolific inventors of our time, Edison changed the world with his inventions of the light bulb, the phonograph, the stock ticker, and the motion picture camera. He held over one thousand national and international patents at his death.

Wilbur Wright - along with his brother Orville, these two changed the world by ushering us into the age of flight. They began their rise to fame as owners of a bicycle shop which provided them some of the components need to perfect their three-axis controls which differentiated their Wright Flyer from others who were attempting to develop a heavier-than-air fixed wing flying machine.

John D. Rockefeller - founder of Standard Oil Company which dominated the petroleum business for years. His business models revolutionized the oil industry and he was also a great philanthropist. He soon became the world's richest person and the first American billionaire. Adjusted for inflation, he is often considered to be the wealthiest person in known history. He spent the final forty years of his life in retirement and his foundations pioneered the development of medical research that lead to the elimination of several diseases. He also founded two well-known universities.

Conclusion

Well - what do you think - fact or fiction? Here are my conclusions.

- Is the Law of Attraction real? Yes - very much so - the evidence is overwhelming!
- Will it work for anyone? Yes, and by extension - everyone!
- Are there any scams about this law? Probably several, so be careful
- Is this a get-rich-quick scheme? No - not at all if presented honestly
- Is it difficult to understand? No - not at all.

- Can I make it work for me? Absolutely - and the rest of this book will help you know exactly how and what to expect each step of the way starting RIGHT NOW!

It's The Law!

Chapter 2
The Law of Attraction
How It Really Works ... Honest! ™

"Like unto like, the thing to the image, the circumstance to the vision, the answer to the prayer - on this law and this law alone areall things constructed, from the atom to the solar system."
- U.S. Andersen

If the Law of Attraction is truly one of God's laws of the universe, it **must** adhere to the same principles governing all of the other laws of the universe. And herein is **the key** to fully understanding and applying this most powerful law successfully. And when you fully understand how it all really works, then you can understand what you need to know to make it work in your daily life for you. You will discover in the following chapters how to harness the power of this amazing law. Once mastered you will be free to change your life forever and make it what you have always wanted it to be. I got so excited when I connected these two dots that you are about to read about that I immediately stopped what I was doing and began to write this book.

The essence of the current focus of Law of Attraction for our purposes here, stated simply, says that you attract into your life what you think about. If you think negative thoughts, you attract into your life what you think about. If you think wealthy thoughts, you attract into your life what you think about. If you think thoughts about being overweight, you attract into your life what you think about. When you stop and consider that - it really makes perfect sense. The physical universe, as quantum mechanics has discovered, is governed by similar relationships of attraction and interconnectivity.

In his book "Three Magic Words", U.S. Andersen made these declarations:

> "We attract into our lives the physical manifestations of the thoughts we think"

> "Through the great law of attraction, all things come to him who believes in them; and every circumstance of your life inevitably has been attracted to you by your own beliefs. You are, literally, a

product of your own thought. You are what you think: only that, nothing more".[3]

That very succinctly describes the workings of the Law of Attraction.

But here is the secret sauce: The Law of Attraction **has** to work in harmony with all other laws of the universe including one of the most prominent and well-known laws - The Laws of the Harvest. When you plant a thought, the universe will respond and you will attract back into your life what you think about, but, and this is a big but, it will come back to you in accordance with the Laws of the Harvest. It can be no other way since these universal laws **must** work in harmony with and **never** contradict each other. There are five Laws of the Harvest which we will now discuss in detail, and you will plainly see how they apply to the Law of Attraction and define its manifestation in your life.

The Laws of the Harvest

Since these are universal laws, you will easily recognize them and your life experience will confirm to you that they are true. If you want to read them, there are several verses in the Bible that refer to these particular laws, although the laws have been in place since the universe began and long before the Bible was written.

The Bible uses them as a simile for spiritual truth that also behaves and abides by these laws. I have included the verses in the bibliography for your reference.

1st Law of the Harvest:
You Reap Only What Has Been Sown

In other words, there has to be a planting before there can be a reaping. This law establishes the relationship and principle of sowing and reaping - reaping is totally dependent upon sowing. Any of you that have planted a garden know that you can't go out to the garden spot and expect something to grow if you haven't first planted it.

How silly then for us to expect a continual and predictable flow of good and wonderful things to surface in our lives until we take time and learn how to properly plant those good and wonderful things. All of these things that we so desperately want in our lives will be reaped if they are properly and continually sown, and being properly sown is foundational to their realization. In Chapter 3 I thoroughly cover how to properly and successfully plant thoughts that will allow the Law of Attraction to work for you.

The important thing at this juncture is to know that planting must occur before reaping can be a reality, and that you are **currently reaping** what you **have been sowing** whether you are aware of it or not. This law, as with all other universal laws, is not dependent upon your knowledge or awareness of it to function. It is constantly and unerringly working behind the scenes twenty four hours per day, seven days per week, and three hundred sixty five days per year.

Whatever your current life circumstance, it is the direct result of the thoughts you have been planting daily over the years, for we are all planting thoughts every day. Now that may not sit well since it limits responsibility to only you for all that is currently in your life. But the good news is, it is also only you who has the power to make the rest of your life whatever you want it to be. *So why not make the rest of your life the best of your life?* No one else has ultimate influence over that. You and you alone control your destiny because your thoughts are uniquely your own. The rest of your life, whether good or bad, is directly in your control since your future thoughts are still future and are yours alone to tender. You are creating your future by what you are thinking every day.

Only you generate and control your thoughts. If you like how your life is currently trending, congratulations! You have been successfully planting thoughts whether you knew exactly how to or not. If you don't like the way your life has been unfolding, the rest of this book will teach you how to change all of that for good. You don't have to continue living a life of unhappiness or scarcity - but how your life history will one day be written is solely in your control.

As it applies to the Law of Attraction, this 1st Law of the Harvest then signifies the launching pad as it is the first step to attracting what you want in your life. You must sow before you can reap, and just as with garden seed, the thoughts you plant have to be planted correctly and nurtured correctly. You reap **only** what has already been sown. It's the law!

2nd Law of the Harvest:
You Reap the Same In Kind As You Sow

In other words, if you plant corn you get corn, not green beans. This is a great law and one of the most important since it guarantees that the labor and effort that you invest into planting will yield exactly and precisely what you are desiring. It provides predictability, hope, and order to the harvest. If you are a farmer and need to plant acres of soy beans to take to market for your livelihood, you certainly don't want to worry about whether lemons will be growing in your field at harvest time! If you need soy beans, you plant soy beans with the absolute knowledge that soy beans will be what grows. Imagine the chaos if you planted corn one year and watermelons appeared. How would anyone ever know what to plant to get what they needed?

This is a powerful law, especially as it applies to the Law of Attraction. If you are serious about making the Law of Attraction your way of life, you need to fully understand this law of the harvest and wrap your mind around it completely. You need to understand it inside-out, upside-down, and front-to-back. You are **guaranteed** that the thoughts that you plant are the **exact and precise reality** that will come back to you - it's **impossible** for it not to or for it to be any other way. Do you realize how powerful that is? Do you? When you master how to successfully plant thoughts, you are **pre-destined** to be what you think about. Just let that sink in for a moment. You are **pre-destined** to be what you think about. Nothing can change or over rule that. It's the law!

I have a good friend from college that has dedicated his life to raising money for foreign missions and he has raised millions of dollars over the past thirty-five years and has had a great impact for the good. He has also been very sick which seemed to start right after college. At last count he has had seventy-three surgeries. Guess what he thinks about all the time? Two things - raising money for missions and how sick he is - seriously! If you were to read his newsletter and summarize its content it talks about those two things. If you were to talk to him in person you would hear the same two things. He is not complaining about being sick all the time, don't misunderstand; he just thinks and talks about it all the time. He is always thanking God for the grace to get through it. It dawned on me after I started to fully understand the Law of Attraction why he is so sick - it's all he thinks about and you attract back into your life what you think about. You reap the *same in kind* as you sow. It's the law!

The 2nd Law of the Harvest will also help you to be specific in your thinking and assist in focusing your thoughts. My first impulse when I fully grasped the power of this law was to plant a multitude of thoughts for everything I ever wanted. I was like a kid in a candy store or a child sitting on Santa's lap before Christmas. The problem soon became that I couldn't remember them all; and are they really thoughts and desires of the heart if you struggle to remember them? I then tried to write them all down and it went from being extreme excitement to being just another big chore. I'm sure many people share that same experience. But just as the farmer usually picks one or two crops to plant every year, this law of the harvest will teach you to focus and be specific about your thoughts as you plant them. They don't all have to be planted at once. You will reap the same in kind as you sow. It's the law!

3rd Law of the Harvest: You Reap In Proportion As You Sow

In other words, if you sow a little, you'll reap a little; and if you sow a lot, you'll reap a lot. This law is also very pivotal to being successful at growing anything. It tells anyone who wants to plant, that if you want a large crop, you have to invest the time and effort and plant proportionally. You can't plant three acres and expect to reap fifty acres. But if you do plant fifty acres, you can realistically expect to reap fifty acres.

Considering this Law of the Harvest in light of the Law of Attraction, you need to plant proportionally to what you want to attract. I'm sure there are many people who have read about the Law of Attraction, gave it a minimal effort, had a modicum of success and chalked it up to just something else that didn't work for them the way they thought. If the Law of Attraction is going to work for you, you must understand this Law of the Harvest and be prepared to invest the level of effort needed to plant the thoughts required to attract into your life what you realistically want to achieve.

Planting three acres is much easier, less costly, and less time consuming than planting fifty acres. But three acres will only bring you three acres of return; and if you truly need and want fifty acres worth of return, then you have to invest whatever is necessary to plant the fifty acres at the outset.

The Law of Attraction works just as advertised, but there are no short cuts. Anything worth having is worth the effort to bring it about. The 3rd Law of the Harvest mandates that the benefits achieved in reaping are directly proportional to the efforts extended in sowing. It can be no other way.

That should not be discouraging, but on the contrary very encouraging. One of the side benefits of the 3rd Law of the Harvest is that it teaches there is **NO LIMIT** to what you can reap. The limit is set by you in the amount that you sow, and we're talking about planting thoughts - not manual labor! That same farmer that planted fifty acres could have just as easily have planted one million acres, and he then would have reaped one million acres of harvest. The limit is set by you, not by the universe. It will always respond in proportion to what you sow with it. You will always reap in proportion to what you sow. Its the law!

4th Law of the Harvest:
You Always Reap More Than You Sow

In other words, if I plant one kernel of corn in the ground properly, I can expect to reap hundreds of times more kernels than I sowed. One kernel of corn will usually yield at least three ears of corn that contain hundreds of individual kernels of corn. What a bonanza! I plant one seed and get hundreds back in return. What type of Wall Street investment matches that? What 401k retirement account offers that rate of return?

According to my research there are an average of 800 kernels which are placed in 16 rows around an average ear of corn. Talk about reaping more than you sow - WOW! Who would even bother to plant anything if all you reaped was the quantity that you sowed?

As you begin to live by the Law of Attraction, this 4th Law of the Harvest will become one of your favorites because it guarantees that whatever thoughts you plant properly will attract an abundance of that thought back into your life. I say properly because if you plant the wrong thoughts they will come back into your life in abundance also. As will be discussed a little later, planting thoughts properly will take some getting used to and shifts in your thinking patterns: but the benefits are, or potentially can be, very overwhelming in the sheer volume of what you reap.

But don't make the mistake of trying to play the numbers game. While a single kernel of corn may return 2,400 kernels in an average, healthy, corn plant; a single apple seed may return up to 800 apples each year and if it lives for thirty years that is 24,000 apples over its life time. In line with that, another truth to keep in mind is that some seeds you plant yield only one crop and other seeds produce a lifetime of crops. So when you are planting thoughts for the Law of Attraction, keep these truths in mind.

The main thing you need to know with this Law of the Harvest is that you will always reap more than you sow and the universe is in charge of how much more. If Mother Nature is any type of indicator of what you can expect, bring a dump truck instead of a gallon bucket!

Perhaps you are like millions who have wondered why their life seems so bad and others seem so good. Here is your answer - you always reap **more** than you sow. Those who plant good thoughts attract an **abundance** of good things back into their life; and those who plant bad thoughts attract an **abundance** of bad things back into their life. Do you see how important this 4th Law of the Harvest is in making the Law of Attraction work the way you want it to work? It works just as advertised - every, single, time. It's the law!

5th Law of the Harvest: You Reap In A Different Season Than You Sow

This law simply declares that when you sow in one season you won't reap until a different, later, season. And the delay in time between planting and reaping is determined by the gestation period of what you have planted. With many common food crops such as sweet corn and green beans it is about three months. With fruit trees it is measured in years.

This 5th Law of the Harvest, in my estimation, is the most important law of all in relation to the Law of Attraction and making it work for you. It is pivotal to your understanding and sensibly managing your expectations. This 5th Law of the Harvest provides a reasonable and logical explanation for the time delay between planting a thought and the time it is attracted back into your life. And knowing people the way I do, this is the area that causes the most frustration. We want everything RIGHT NOW!

Over the past sixty years or so, our society has taken a very significant shift. My parent's generation was not driven by demands of instant gratification, but rather they were content to work hard, and allow things to come in their natural course.

That all began to change dramatically with the introduction of television in the late 40's and early 50's when highly visual commercials for a wide variety of products were beamed into our homes. That was followed by easier credit and the advent of the credit card. If you didn't have the cash on hand - no worry - just charge it. Throw in fast food restaurants and HAVE IT NOW quickly became the mantra.

The disconnect is that societal evolution has no effect on the laws of the universe - they are immutable and just keep plodding along at their normal, predictable pace, totally oblivious to the impatience of our current generation. The Laws of the Harvest work the same every time.

I can imagine that many people read about the Law of Attraction, decide to give it a try, plant some thoughts, and then give up and go back to their default way of thinking after a very short period of time with no results thinking it doesn't work for them. They think they have wasted their money on another scheme that only serves to make the author wealthy.

This 5th Law of the Harvest is the missing link that will help you understand the need to expect a delay between planting and reaping, and it is a delay you have already experienced in your life and fully understand. Everyone has either planted a garden or been near farm crops and is aware of planting season and harvest season. We even have such terms as a harvest moon, and holidays and festivals based upon these two different and celebrated seasons.

It is not God or the universe ignoring or denying you, it is the natural universal sequence of events associated with planting and reaping, playing out in front of you on life's stage, and it is true for everything that is planted and harvested in any fashion. In this culture of instant gratification, waiting for something to materialize is an unpopular concept; but as the adage goes, good things come to those who wait. But the wait is more tolerable when it is expected, well defined, and understood.

What everyone who wants to be successful with the Law of Attraction needs to understand and get your mind around is that it works in accordance with the Laws of the Harvest - especially this one. When you plant a thought, there will be an indeterminate interval of time before it is attracted back into your life; and that time interval between planting and reaping - whether short or long - is wholly dependent upon the universe's schedule. You can't hurry it up or slow it down - all you can do is patiently wait and continue to hold the thought. If it is important enough to plant in the first place, its resultant attraction back into your life is well worth the time interval required - whatever it may be.

A good example of that is a personal story conveyed by John Assaraf in the book "The Secret" by Rhonda Byrne:

> "Knowing the law of attraction, I wanted to really put it to use and to see what would happen. In 1995 I started to create something called a Vision Board, where I take something that I want to achieve, or something that I want to attract, like a car or a watch or the soul mate of my dreams, and I put a picture of what I want up on this board. Every day I would sit in my office and I would look up at this board and I would start to visualize. I would really get into the state of having already acquired it.
>
> I was getting ready to move. We put all of the furniture, all of the boxes, into storage, and I made three different moves

over a period of five years. And then I ended up in California and bought this house, renovated it for a year, and then had all the stuff brought from my former home five years earlier. One morning my son Keenan came into my office, and one of the boxes that was sealed for years was right at the doorstep. He asked, "What's in the boxes, Daddy?" And I said, "Those are my Vision Boards." He then asked, "What's a Vision Board?" I said, "Well, it's where I put all my goals up. I cut them out and I put all my goals up as something that I want to achieve in my life." Of course at five and a half years old he didn't understand, and so I said, "Sweetheart, let me just show you, that'll be the easiest way to do it."

I cut the box open, and one Vision Board was a picture of a home that I was visualizing five years earlier. What was shocking was that we were living in that house. Not a house like it - I actually bought my dream home, renovated it, and didn't even know it. I looked at that house and I started to cry, because I was just blown away. Keenan asked, "Why are you crying?" "I finally understand how the law of attraction works. I finally understand the power of visualization. I finally understand everything that I've read, everything that I've worked with my whole life, the way I've built companies. It worked for my home as well, and I bought our dream home and didn't even know it."[4]

Don't make the mistake of trying to determine the length of time between thought and reality based upon your assessment of the size or complexity of the content of the thought. It is no harder for a new car to be attracted into your life than for a bicycle to be attracted into your life. We're dealing with a God who creates worlds! And he makes no mistakes. Attracting money, or homes, or cars, or whatever your thoughts center on into your life is not a matter that will tax his ability to be sure, but the universe will answer back in its time frame alone. But you must leave the "how" in God's hands and stop trying to guess how he's going to accomplish it or trying to help him along. He's able all by himself and will gladly show you that if you'll let him.

Realize the truthfulness of this 5th Law of the Harvest and keep thinking those good thoughts. At least now you know why there is a delay, can expect it to be there every time you plant thoughts, and can understand what it is all about. Over time you will actually learn how to use it to your advantage and be able to plan ahead. The message here is you will always reap in a different season than you sow. It's the law!

While the most reported areas are finance, health, jobs, homes, cars, etc. there are no boundaries on the type of thoughts that you can plant with the Law of Attraction. Use your imagination or look deep into your heart - whatever you can think about can become a candidate for this law. Some use it to find romance, others use it to develop a career. Even others have used it to advance at their job with a promotion. There is nothing too large or too small, too strange or too normal for this law. I personally used it to obtain the condo I wanted and currently reside in when I accepted the new job that I had brought into my life by using this law. Be adventurous! Dream big! Dare to step out! Even the sky is no limit for this law!

Summary

To summarize, in this chapter you have learned that the Law of Attraction works seamlessly with and is dependent upon the Laws of the Harvest to determine the way thoughts are manifested back into your life. These laws are immutable and state

1. You reap only what has already been sown
2. You reap the same in kind as you sow
3. You reap in proportion as you sow
4. You reap more than you sow
5. You reap in a different season than you sow

It's The Law!

Chapter 3
Creating Proper Thoughts For The Law of Attraction

"To reach a higher level of being, you must assume a higher concept of yourself" - Neville Goddard

Without debate, the most important part of successfully deploying the Law of Attraction into your life is knowing that the thoughts you are planting will, in-fact, yield the results that you desire. Unfortunately, it is easy to do the wrong thing, end up frustrated, and give up. There is no magic formula here nor is there a manual written in some ancient manuscript that defines clearly how to proceed, just some good common sense guidelines and logical reasoning. Remember, God wants you to succeed because this Law of Attraction did not originate with any human being; it is a universal law that originated with the intelligence that created the universe. It has been in operation for thousands of years, and many people just like you have successfully deployed it in their lives. It has been at work behind the scenes whether you knew it or not.

There are some individual principles involved in the overall process that when taken collectively give a clearer picture of what is required and I have listed them here at the outset. In order to manifest in a material form the things you wish to create the following need to be achieved:

1. You must continually plant specific thoughts about what you want to attract into your life.
2. You must "think from the end" and imagine the thought as though it were already a completed action including feeling what it will feel like when it is reality.
3. You must express gratitude for the thought as though it were already done.

Now let's look at them in greater detail.

Planting Specific Thoughts

The Law of Attraction uses your thoughts as its call to action and marching orders. It stands idly by until you call it into action. You call it into action by actively and purposely thinking and rigorously focusing your mind on whatever it is that you want to attract into your life. The cautionary note here is that this law knows no difference between what is bad for you and what is good for you. It is a predictable, impartial, non-personal law that operates the same way every time no matter whom it is serving, and obeys specific conditions without regards to consequences for you. You are the one who owns your thoughts and as such you have sole control over their content. You are therefore also the one who is totally responsible for their content and ramifications in your life. You are at choice to think whatever you choose at any given moment. That is why you need to be specific and focused on what you truly want to create.

Let me give you a personal example of how easy it is to get your mind on something and not be able to move it off. I was driving on an interstate highway just the other day on a beautiful sunny morning. It was the third day of fall and the sky was a deep beautiful blue. As I was driving, as often is my practice, I was spending some time in meditation, thinking from the end about some thoughts I had planted, and assuming the role of the person I wanted to become. I was having a wonderful time, I was feeling very good, and just enjoying the time alone with my thoughts.

All of a sudden, a yellow warning light on the dashboard illuminated and I glanced down to see what it was. For whatever reason my car has warning lights with both the US and Canadian standard - I am guessing the car was made in Canada originally and the

Canadian ones are usually a symbol with no words and they are the ones that always show up when one illuminates. It appeared to be telling me that I had low tire pressure in a tire. First of all, I didn't even know my ten-year-old car was equipped with tire pressure sensors, secondly, I had just had the tires checked and rotated about a month before and they had been fine, and they only had about 15,000 miles on them since new. I kept driving, but my eyes kept glancing at that light and my mind was in overdrive. Was there really a problem? Would I have a blowout and lose control soon? Which tire was it? Maybe it's two tires. Maybe it's all four tires! Maybe I ran over something and didn't know it. I kept driving. I let go of the steering wheel temporarily to try to determine if one of the front tires was low - nothing - it tracked perfectly straight. There was an exit about three miles up the road and I decided to stop and check to make sure there was nothing wrong.

As I exited the car I glanced at all four tires as I made my way around it and sure enough - all four tires were fine. Whew! I was glad there was nothing wrong, partially because I had a trunk full of items I was moving and getting to the spare would have been a challenge. I made a call while I was stopped, got a soft drink and hopped back in to the car. As I started the engine, the light came back on immediately. I again got out and looked to see if perhaps one of them was even a little low - nope - all was just fine. I hopped back into the car and resumed my journey. But the light never went out and as I travelled for the next twenty miles of my journey, I kept glancing at that light from time-to-time and trying to resume my meditation and thought planting. But my mind was having none of that - it was fixated on that little yellow light and it was all I could think about.

And then it dawned on me - in a flash it was painfully apparent to me that this little light had stolen my total attention; I was no longer able to meditate and do what I had been doing and I was totally mesmerized by it. The sensor was probably just faulty and yet I couldn't let it go - even though I knew better. Trying as hard as I could to concentrate on something else - anything else - I failed and it had me totally under its spell.

And then in a moment that I can only describe as an awakening, it was as if someone had taken a large marker and written across the sky "this is how bad thoughts can take over your mind and the Law of Attraction works in these instances too".

We've all been there - driving when a warning light comes on or another type of critical interruption occurs - your mind just takes on a life of its own and you seem totally powerless to do much of anything about it. But you must take back control and re-focus your attention on what you really want to attract back into your life. I did it that day by starting the CD player and listening to one of Dr. Wayne Dyer's CDs. In just a few short moments, I was back in control.

But with the thousands of thoughts flooding your mind daily from all regions of your consciousness, does the Law of Attraction work on every single thought you have? My answer to that is no. It only works on the thoughts that you focus strongly on and decide to take to the next level which is thinking from the end. Not every thought I have through the day do I advance to steps two and three of the process. That takes focus and effort, and in my estimation that is where the separation exists. Thoughts will become things but only when you work through the entire process.

In his book "The Power of Awareness" Neville Goddard puts it this way.

> "... for an idea is endowed with power only in proportion to the degree of attention fixed on it".[5]

If you will take an honest inventory of your life right now it will reflect the things that you have thought about with great focus and feeling in the past. You may not even have realized how much you were thinking about specific things. We tend to obsess about things at times, especially extreme things in our life, and that qualifies as rigorous focus and feeling. Thinking to a point of obsession about the things you don't like in your life or the things that are causing you great stress and anxiety is very common. Unfortunately, when these become your prolonged focus, you attract more if it back into your life, and the time delay is almost nonexistent since, in essence, it is just more of what is already there.

On a practical level, if you are just beginning to consciously use the Law of Attraction an important thing to consider is limiting yourself to one thought at-a-time until that one is accomplished. Your thought must also be very specific since you will need to focus intensely on it. By specific I mean detailed. If you plan to plant a thought about a vehicle for instance, you need to be very specific about that vehicle - what brand is it, what color is it, what year is it, what date do you want it by, etc.

Back in 1971 I was attending Bible College and needed a car so I began to intensely pray about that car which is certainly a method of planting thoughts, even though I was ignorant of the Law of Attraction at that time. In my mind I was trying to impress God and not seem like I needed the best car so my thoughts were along the lines of low mileage, built very well, not necessarily very new or real recent - nothing fancy - basically just your average car. I was trying to be spiritual you know and I didn't need the best. Well, I got exactly what I asked for. A man in the church I was attending came to me one day and said "I understand you need a car, and I have one you can have. It's nothing special for sure but it runs and it's free".

Nothing special was an understatement to be sure. The car was a 1960 model MG Magnette that had the trunk smashed in a bit but was still drivable; it had low miles, was built like a Sherman tank, got great mileage, had a terrible paint job, and one other thing - no starter. There was a place for one but it was missing. But, it had a hand crank that was used to start the engine. Imagine me pulling up in front of a church where I was to be a guest speaker, trying to be real spiritual and when the service was over going out and crank-starting my car! I learned a very valuable lesson to be very specific in the thoughts that you plant.

On the matter of limiting yourself, your natural instinct will be to "go for the gusto" and try to do too many thoughts at once. There is no hurry and this law will be functioning tomorrow as well as today. If you're like me and have spent a lot of years in ignorance you want to make up for lost time; and worse yet, you fear God may turn it off before you get all your thoughts in line. That's not going to happen so just relax and enjoy this law. It is better that you go slowly and learn exactly what it takes to positively activate it in your life and then add more thoughts. Your success will encourage you to use it even more and will provide you with insight into how it specifically works for you. You have already experienced through ignorance of this law the unfavorable results it can yield. Take the time to learn to use it correctly, and start slowly to turn your life around.

Most people use this law to change things they don't like in their life whether that is their job, their home, their car, their finances, their health, or any number of other things. Ironically, the things they don't like in their life are probably there because of this same law - they focused on the things they didn't want and that is what they attracted back into their life surreptitiously using this law.

Along this same line, your thoughts need to be about what you **do** want rather than what you **don't** want - the positive rather than the negative. The Law of Attraction is all about creating what **you want** by attracting back into your life what your thoughts are focused on. You can probably think of hundreds of things that you don't want, but if you want to change your life don't go there. What **do** you want - be specific? This is not always as easy as it first sounds.

True confession time. When I first began living this philosophy and actively engaging this law, this was, and still is, my hardest task - getting specific about what *I* really want. I had been taught all my life that others had to come first, that what I wanted was always secondary, and so consequently I never thought much about what I really wanted. Years of parental teaching and up-bringing followed by four years of Bible College re-affirming that others must always come first had taken its mental toll. Even at Christmas as a child, the under-privileged had to be thought of first and what I wanted was somewhere after that. I had to first of all get to the point where I would allow myself to even believe it was OK for me think about what *I* wanted. Believe me, that took quite a while but I finally got there through many struggles. Changing a life-long mindset is not done overnight, but the good news is, it *can* be done.

So take whatever time is necessary and develop a blueprint of what you truly want to create in your life. Organize this plan into logical smaller steps of priority which will then be your master list for thoughts to plant. As each thought is planted, manifested, and successfully realized you move on to the next one. This, then will become your goal and sole focus as you move forward with the Law of Attraction.

You will notice early on that several things are happening simultaneously. As you systematically create your blueprint you will be generating positive thoughts about yourself and your future and you will immediately begin to feel good. This is a good thing. As you continue to feel good, your view of what you want to create will become clearer and your thoughts will become more focused. As you slowly watch thoughts become things, you will gain confidence in yourself and this law and you will notice that one of the side benefits is that negative things in your life will begin to fade away. You will realize that you are doing the right things and that the Law of Attraction is working with you as your partner instead of working against you.

Now I'm going to give you a very important truth about planting thoughts in your life and it is very pivotal to your success. If you don't get anything else out of this particular section, make sure you get this.

I'm not sure how many people outside of agriculture know this, but when you plant a seed in the ground, before it can take root, germinate, and bring forth its bounty - it must literally die. That's right - it must die.

The bible alludes to this truth in John 12:24 (KJV) where it says:

> "Except a corn of wheat fall into the ground and die, it abideth alone; but if it die it brings forth much fruit".

Clearly then, if it doesn't die it will never grow or produce anything. Likewise, you must be willing to die to whatever it is that you want to change in your life if your thoughts are to be successful using the Law of Attraction. You can't plant a thought of accumulating wealth and still think and feel like you're poor, even if you are. You can't plant a thought of achieving your perfect goal weight if you constantly act and talk as if you're fat - even if you are. You must die to that old thought pattern that has plagued you all your life. Ironic isn't it - death must occur for new life to begin.

You may ask "How do I die to my old thought patterns?" When you realize the essence of the meaning of death it will become apparent. Death, in its fullest and most present impact, is a separation. Whatever dies is separated from whatever is left behind alive. When a person dies, while their spirit is eternally alive, it is no longer present in the body as the person we knew and loved - it is gone - separated from us. When a beloved pet dies, the spirit and personality of that animal that we loved and that gave so much love and joy back to us is gone - separated from us. We cry and grieve because of this absence and separation and the great feeling of loss that we experience.

In the same way, you must learn to separate yourself completely and permanently from your former thought pattern or mindset. Only by dying to your old thought patterns can you invoke the power of the Law of Attraction to create a new life for yourself. And isn't that what this is all about - attracting into your life the good things you wish to create instead of more of what has been plaguing you?

Thinking from the End

In his book "The Power of Awareness", Neville Goddard makes the following observation.

> "You must imagine that you are already experiencing what you desire".[5]

The thought here is profound yet quite simple - you must act as if what you want has already happened. Feel it! Smell it! Hear the sounds of it! Touch it! Imagine yourself having it! Make it real in your mind. This is called thinking from the end.

Notice it is not thinking ABOUT the end but thinking FROM the end. There is a great difference and it is identical in performance and function to the bible doctrine of believing faith. That doctrine holds that faith is simply believing that what has not yet happened will certainly happen and is on its way.

Businesses do this all the time. They have five-year plans, ten-year plans whatever the time frame may be and what they are doing is asking themselves "where do we want to be in five years or ten years?" They then set out a course, thinking from the end about what they intend to achieve, and make business decisions accordingly. Steve Jobs, the late CEO of Apple was a master at it. He spent the latter and most productive part of his stellar business career thinking from the end. It lead him to such great things as the iPod, iPhone, iPad, and changed the way we listen to and buy our music today and probably for years to come. It transformed a common cell phone into the most valuable and useful tool we own. Apple stock has gone from $15 per share when he returned to Apple in the late 90's to over $700 per share the week this was written. Planting thoughts and thinking from the end is real and it works no matter where you apply it. And it will work for you too.

Also in the business world in Lean Manufacturing, one of the main concepts of Lean Product Development is project planning that in essence employs thinking from the end. Traditional project plans start with today and then add specific tasks to be accomplished along with an estimate of required completion time. When all the tasks are listed the time is added up and a finish date is established.

The Lean method establishes the completion date first based upon customer demands and market trends and then systematically adds tasks working backwards toward the current date. In this way, delivery dates are strategic and met with regularity rather than left to the whims of chance.

This is the epitome of thinking from the end in a business setting, for as you work this plan you must ask yourself if I am going to have product ready to ship on this date, what has to be done the day before that to ensure I can ship product? And then what has to be done the day before that, and the day before that and so on?

Once you begin to think and plan this way, it will become apparent that this is a great tool. Having learned it in business, I now use it for just about everything in my life. I used it in writing this book and will do so for every book. The simplest and most effective way is to make a board to hang on a wall, list dates across the top and place sticky notes with detailed tasks under the completion dates required to achieve your goal. Work it from right to left - completion date to current date.

The way to think from the end is quite simple but takes some getting used to for most people. You have to learn to frame future events in the present tense. Here's an example. Instead of planting the thought "I want a new truck" - reframe it this way "I am the owner of a new, black, Ford F150". When you think "I want ..." the Law of Attraction will bring "I want" back into your life and you will always be in a state of wanting. That's a necessary shift in the way you think and it is also quite important.

Now notice also how specific that is. Can you see it? Can you smell that new car smell? Reach out and touch it in your mind! What do you look like sitting inside! What does the dash look like! What does the engine sound like as it roars to life! As you leave the dealership, where is your first destination! Who is sitting beside you as you drive? You were right there inside that new truck weren't you? With a little practice and shifting your mind to believe it is real and on its way by use of your imagination and visualization, you will quickly learn how to frame future events in the present tense and master thinking from the end.

I can hear many of you saying "Well that's telling a lie, I don't have a new vehicle". That is YOUR thought that's in YOUR mind alone, that YOU are planting - you don't tell other people what you are planting unless they understand what you are doing with the Law of Attraction.

Hebrews 11:1 (CEB) says:

> "Faith is the **reality** of what we hope for and the **proof** of things not yet seen. (Emphasis mine)

That seems pretty clear.

As I wrap up this section and as an illustration of this principle allow me to relate to you a brief synopsis of how I am thinking from the end about a specific thought I am currently planting. I have planted several specific thoughts since learning of the Law of Attraction all of which have manifested flawlessly - this is my current one. And it is, by far, the largest and most complex thought from a human perspective.

I am an avid boater and have been wanting to upgrade to a little larger boat since I plan to make it my home when I retire. It is my intention to retire from my engineering career soon, be fully engaged in my writing career, live on my boat, and spend the summers writing while I am cruising the Great Lakes starting next summer in Lake Huron.

My current situation is that I am employed full time as an engineering manager coming home only on the weekends from a job that is more than two-hundred miles away from my home. I own a very nice mid-sized boat and while being within months of full retirement age, have no means to retire anytime soon due to the continuing economic downturn and a 401k that tanked as a result of it. So the thoughts I am planting represent a total shift from my present reality - a perfect candidate for the Law of Attraction.

I have already planned my travel itinerary in advance for next summer's three month cruise, assigning dates to specific destinations, and carefully charting my course. Drawing upon my previous cruising experiences I plan to spend a week at each port-of-call, and have set my itinerary for sixteen weeks beginning the Friday before the Memorial Day holiday and ending the week after the Labor Day holiday.

Twice a week during my three hour, two hundred mile commute in the privacy and quietness of my car, in my mind I visualize myself leaving one port and traveling to the next port. Today I am traveling from East Tawas, MI to Alpena, MI, and I carefully and methodically go through each item on my departure check list while getting the boat ready to leave port. In my mind I see all of the docks, the other boats tied up nearby, and the dock hands who have helped me cast off the lines waving goodbye as I back out of my slip. I can even see the expressions on their faces. I smell the diesel exhaust and the fresh coffee I have brewed, feel the gentle breeze as the sun gently chases away the chill of the early spring morning, and hear the familiar haunting screech of sea gulls as they opportunistically scan the waters below in search of their first meal of the day. I take note of the minor chop created by the onshore breeze as I round the break wall and head out to open waters. I hear the engines roar to life as I advance the throttles, the stern settles gently downward, the bow rises to meet the horizon, and the boat climbs up on plane. As I head into another picturesque and memorable sunrise, the sun glistens and dances atop the crests of the rippling waves.

In my mind, I visualize every turn, every scene of nature along the shoreline, every setting on the GPS, every reading on the engine gages, every other vessel on the water, and even the cormorants and sea gulls as they follow the fishing boats. I hear conversations on the marine radio and observe the current weather reports en route. And when I get to my new destination, in my mind I visualize every step and maneuver required as I bring my new boat to her new home for the next week.

I do two ports-of-call each week while driving until I get through the entire itinerary and then I start all over again. It usually takes about forty-five minutes from beginning to end. I visualize all of the specific sights, smell all of the smells, hear all of the sounds, think all of the thoughts, and feel all of the feelings associated with each event. I can imagine myself on the bridge fully engaged in my new career and life.

It is so real that when I am done I feel as though I have actually been there and lived the experience already. In my thoughts there have been times when I was fishing off of the bow of the boat and I could actually feel the fish tugging on the line as he fought to stay away from the boat. In my thoughts I have rowed to shore, climbed the beautiful red quartz rocks, walked among the trees on the bluffs of the Benjamin Islands, and smelled the fresh fragrance of virgin pines that have never been approached by a human due to their remoteness. In my thoughts I have sat in restaurants and met people who I full well expect to meet when the trip actually occurs next summer. On one occasion in Little Current, Ontario there was a married couple from Oregon just walking up and down the dock looking at the boats. In my thoughts they had both read my book, recognized me from the book jacket, and wanted to tell me their thoughts about it. Your imagination is a wonderful and powerful tool essential to your ability to successfully think from the end.

And at the end of each session of thinking from the end, I spend time expressing genuine, heart-felt gratitude, for I visualize it all as current reality and having already happened. It is my intention to do this relentlessly until the reality is manifested.

An Attitude of Gratitude

This final step in planting proper thoughts is very important to understand and master. You must learn to genuinely give thanks for everything that comes your way - no matter what it is. That's right NO MATTER WHAT IT IS! To be sure, not all of these things are what you have brought into your life by your past thoughts through the Law of Attraction. We must realize that there are circumstances in life that just happen, that are out of our control, and you must learn to give thanks for them whether you want to or not. Why do you suppose this step is even here? There are three very good reasons if you are serious about making the Law of Attraction a way of life for you.

First of all it brings you to the realization that everything that happens in your life is on purpose and intended and specifically designed for you by the all-knowing creative mind who put you here. He knows all and knows what's best for all of us and faithfully parades that into our lives a day-at-a-time.

That school bus that pulled out in front of you that will probably stop five times and may cause you to be late to work is just exactly what you needed - genuinely give thanks for it! The clogged toilet that caused water to overflow all over the floor was exactly what you needed - genuinely give thanks for it! That $20 bill you found on the ground at the mall parking lot was just exactly what you needed - genuinely give thanks for it.

And if when you first start this process the gratitude is not quite yet genuine, mouth the words and say them anyway; they will become genuine as you truly realize that the creative force who put you here knows best for you and makes no mistakes. He knows exactly what you need and when you need it and his faithfulness to the objects of his affection causes him to bring that into your life in little daily doses so that you are never overwhelmed - even though at times you may feel like you are. As one of my professors used to say "If you feel like you're at the end of your rope, tie a knot and hang on". Have a genuine attitude of gratitude for everything that comes your way - it is on purpose and in your best interest.

I came across a poem titled "Don't Quit" by an unknown author years ago that seems quite appropriate here.

> "When things go wrong, as they
> sometimes will,
> When the road you're trudging seems
> all uphill,
> When the funds are low and the debts
> are high,
> And you want to smile, but you have to
> sigh,
> When care is pressing you down a bit,
> Rest, if you must, but don't you quit.
>
> Life is queer with its twists and turns,
> As every one of us sometimes learns,
> And many a failure turns about,
> When he might have won had he stuck it
> out;
> Don't give up though the pace seems

slow-You may succeed with another
blow.

Often the goal is nearer than,
It seems to a faint and faltering man,
Often the struggler has given up,
When he might have captured the
victor's cup,
And he learned too late when the night
slipped down,
How close he was to the golden crown.

Success is failure turned inside out-The
silver tint of the clouds of doubt,
And you never can tell how close you are,
It may be near when it seems so far,
So stick to the fight when you're hardest
hit--
It's when things seem worst that you
mustn't quit"

Secondly, if you can learn to genuinely give thanks for
whatever shows up in your daily life, nothing can defeat
or derail you as you parlay the Law of Attraction into
your own personal success story. If you're going to learn
how to plant thoughts and use the Law of Attraction
successfully, you need to learn just how easy it is to get
your mind on the wrong thing and the ramifications of

leaving it there. Genuinely giving thanks will dissolve the momentary anger or frustration you may sense as an unexpected and unwanted event surfaces in your life. How bad can it be if you can genuinely give thanks for it?

Plus that, even though many of the things we're discussing here are just life happening on a daily basis, some of what is showing up in your life is the direct result of the thoughts you have been planting, so why not give thanks - after all **you** placed the order for it, the universe is merely responding and bringing into your life what you said you wanted.

I'll admit that this was a hard one for me because by nature I tend to be very, very, impatient. This was brought home to me in a most unflattering way many years ago. One early evening when my middle son was about three, we were in the car driving to the grocery store which happened to be in another town about twelve miles away. It was back in the days before children had to be in car seats and he was standing in the front seat right between my wife and me. The speed limit on the rural country road was fifty-five and there was a car in front of us going about forty or so. My wife and I were talking quietly and all of a sudden out of nowhere he blurts out quite loudly "What's the matter lady, don't you know how to drive"? Well ... there was a dead silence in the car for what seemed forever and my wife looked at me and said "Well I wonder where he learned that"? BUSTED!!!

At that time I hated waiting in line for anything which is a daily occurrence for most of us. To me waiting in line was piddling your life away one second at-a-time while doing nothing. I would always imagine what I could have been doing instead of wasting my time in line, which usually made it worse, and I also felt that it was an insult by the establishment causing the line. They apparently didn't want to spend the money to hire more people to take care of the level of patronage that they had. They were perfectly comfortable with me wasting my life. How could I ever be thankful for that?

Now when I see lines somewhere that I must get into, I try to get in the longest one and practice giving thanks until I reach the front. I wondered at first what I could possibly learn to be thankful for while waiting in a line. And as I began to stand in the lines I took notice of the expressions on the faces of all of those in line with me and I decided to use the time to start conversations with others standing there and sharing my plight. What a great experience that has been. What I thought I had been wasting - my time - actually turned out to be a great investment in new friendships and relationships. I have met some really great people just waiting in line and I can now genuinely give thanks when I enter a line because I know I'm about to meet some new people who are supposed to be in my life. A thing of drudgery has turned into a thing of joy. Genuine gratitude comes more quickly and easily for me now.

I recently discovered an amazing gem - expressing gratitude also provides me a convenient platform to show kindness to everyone I encounter which is a personal goal I have set for myself. Now when a truck pulls out in front of me, instead of getting upset at the impending delays, I give thanks that the situation has provided an opportunity to show kindness to the driver since he is just like me and doing what he feels is best for him at that time. It is not my job to judge, condemn, or criticize other people who share the planet with me.

I may lose some of you right here on this third item. After you read this item, you may put this book down and never pick it up again thinking I just can't do that - not right now anyhow. And I fully realize that. But this third item about giving thanks is as important as the first two and needs to be addressed. If I lose you, I trust that at a later time you will be able to pick this up and go on where you left off because the benefits to be gained far outweigh the anguish and pain you are feeling as you think about these things.

Thirdly, giving thanks will help you to find beauty in things that you may normally despise. Where is the beauty in a drunken driver going the wrong way at night on an interstate highway and crashing head-on into a minivan and killing a precious family of four with two young children? Where is the beauty in a child being born with fetal alcohol syndrome and destined for a life of struggle? Where is the beauty in a spouse or other life partner deciding they want to be with someone else now, after decades together, and no longer with you? Where is the beauty in the vibrant life of a young soldier with a spouse and new baby at home being cut short thousands of miles away from home in some far-off distant land trying to protect people who don't even want them there in the first place because of a senseless, political war?

These are all very, very hard questions that life brings upon us daily. And yes, as hard as it will seem, we all must learn to see the beauty in them, for there is beauty to be found, and be able to give genuine thanks for these tragedies that befall us.

You may well say, I can see no beauty whatsoever in that, and there is no way I could ever give thanks; and if there were a God in heaven, He would never allow such things to happen to begin with! I've heard that for years from the lips of countless grieving hearts. And I fully understand it. But may I suggest to you that the beauty lies in learning to give love where you want to give hatred, and granting forgiveness where you want to invoke judgment.

Forgiveness must be granted, for without it these things will clog your mind and cause hatred and bitterness that will eat away at you like a moth eating fabric; and it will eat at you until you are totally consumed in bitterness. When you can genuinely forgive, then you will begin to see the beauty, and when you begin to see the beauty you will begin to genuinely give thanks. I know it's hard, but I also know it can be done because it has happened to me and I have done it.

Mark Twain wrote the following about forgiveness.

> "Forgiveness is the fragrance that the
> violet sheds on the heel that crushed it"[6]

I can't read, think, or say that out loud without tears welling up in my eyes. The beauty of the metaphor is over-powering to me - I break down just about every time. What a wonderful framing of the principle of forgiveness.

To summarize this section, if you purpose to be successful with the Law of Attraction, you will need to learn to plant specific thoughts, think from the end, and have an attitude of gratitude. When you do, there is no limit to what you can create.

It's The Law!

Chapter 4
Preparing For the Harvest

"The thankful receiver bears a plentiful harvest."
- William Blake

Many people think that there is nothing to do between planting a thought and reaping the result which is manifesting it back into your life as reality. Just ask any farmer or occasional gardener and they will tell you that there is plenty yet to be done. And preparing for the harvest is the really fun and exciting part, because you know that your bountiful harvest is on its way and you are making preparation to receive it. You are also taking some precautionary steps to protect your investment.

I remember my grandmother putting out a small garden in her back yard every year. I was too young to know much about what was going on, but I remember that she would get all excited as "picking time", as she put it, was nigh. She made me help her get out the canning jars and some large pottery crocks that seemed to weigh as much as an elephant. She would get everything cleaned up, in its place, and ready for picking time. She thoroughly loved her little vegetable garden and I loved the many delicious dishes she used to fix for me when I went to visit her.

Since we have established that all of the laws of the universe must work in concert with each other and that none may contradict, and that the Law of Attraction must work in harmony with the Laws of the Harvest, it follows then that whatever is planted must receive timely and incremental attention if it is to flourish and produce the intended result. Much of this attention is provided by nature itself, but the farmer or occasional gardener who purposes to be successful is ready to provide the needed attention should nature not provide it. Let's examine some of these.

Watering the Seed

The seed that a farmer plants must receive water if it is going to grow and produce the intended result. The bulk of this water comes in the form of rainfall that is the natural result of normal climactic activity. There is a "window" of acceptable amounts of moisture for proper growth - too much and you'll drown the plant - too little and it will starve; either way it is dead and will not produce the intended result.

In like manner, you need to take time to "water" your thoughts after they are planted. By that I mean, continue to daily think from the end and feel yourself being in the condition that you have intended. Continue to assume the role of your intentions being completed, as though it was already done, and give them the proper amount of attention. After all, you are saying to the universe by planting them that this is what you want to attract back into your life. Doesn't it make sense then that you need to continue to think very strongly about your intended result everyday - meditate on it and let it consume you? You may be wondering "how long do I need to think from the end?" My motto is "Think from the end till you get to the end"!

I love to watch children at Christmas time. They are perfect examples of this very principle. Do you think that they make a list of what they want for Christmas, give it to you, and then just forget about it? Everyone who has children knows that they become obsessed with it, they never stop thinking about it, and their every conversation seems to always work its way around to what they want for Christmas. And as parents who have purchased the items and already know that their wishes are soon to be fulfilled, we watch them with great joy and occasionally tease them about this or that knowing full well that we have allowed their wish to be our command. Half the fun of Christmas is watching your kids plant their thoughts, cultivate and water their thoughts, and then see their expressions of joy and amazement when the sacred day arrives. We even at times wrap the gifts and place them under the tree in advance which gives them a preview of things to come and increases the excitement all the more.

It's the same with God and the universe - they take great delight in clandestinely observing you thinking and meditating daily about what it is that you want to manifest all the while knowing that it is on its way to you. They love watching you imagine what the intention fulfilled will be like and feeling those feelings when you have actually received back into your life what you have planted. They watch quietly as you assume the role of the intention fulfilled and feel the enjoyment of what you have manifested through the Law of Attraction. Nothing delights God more than doting on and providing for his children.

They also give you a preview; for whatever is planted in nature produces evidence that it is alive and growing no matter what it is. When a kernel of corn is planted properly it isn't long until a small sprout appears popping its head through the ground. When a child is conceived, it isn't long until that little maternal bulge appears. That evidence is there to keep you encouraged in your quest. It is also a harbinger that more attention will be required ahead.

Neville Goddard talks about what he calls the Law of Assumption in his book "The Power of Awareness". Notice these isolated statements.

> "By assuming the idea already to be a fact, it is converted into reality."

> "You must assume that you are what you want to be and continue therein ..."

> "Your assumption, to be effective, cannot be a single isolated act; it must be a maintained attitude of the wish fulfilled. [And that maintained attitude that gets you there, so that you think from your wish fulfilled instead of thinking about your wish, is aided by assuming the feeling of the wish fulfilled frequently. It is the frequency, not the length of time, that makes it natural. That to which you constantly return constitutes your truest self. Frequent occupancy of the feeling of the wish fulfilled is the secret of success.]"[5]

He's not talking about making an assumption as in guessing, but rather assuming a role. For example "He assumed the role of the doctor in the play". So after you plant your thought and begin to think from the end, assume the role of the intention fulfilled.

And as you assume the role of whatever your heart has purposed, you are creating daily evidence of the thought fulfilled; and it is hard evidence that you actually feel and experience. All of life has evidence of its existence and this same evidence serves as proof of reality.

Removing the Weeds

Everyone who has ever planted a garden knows that weeds grow all on their own and if you don't stay on top of their removal, they will choke your young plants and they will die. If left totally unchecked, they will ravenously take over the entire garden and all you will have is a bountiful harvest of weeds.

Weeds are a very interesting phenomenon since they spring up all on their own - no one goes into the garden and plants them - and they are very difficult to kill. They can survive on very little water, have roots that extend very deeply into the soil, and they multiply very quickly. Farmers use sophisticated herbicides that are applied in differing ways to head off weed development in their fields. They also use crop dusters when needed to spray their fields when things are getting out of control.

The weeds that threaten to kill your harvest come in the form of doubts that crop up in your mind all on their own and are difficult to chase away. As you devotedly and systematically plant specific thoughts, purpose to think from the end, and stay in an attitude of gratitude, these pesky doubts will appear out of nowhere as if guided by a laser beam penetrating deep into the innermost chambers of your mind and heart where only you live. They will cause discouragement by whispering to you that nothing is really happening, that nothing is on its way to you as you've been lead to believe, and that you've made a big fool of yourself - AGAIN! They will continue to whisper that the Law of Attraction is a con, just the demented musing of some huckster's imagination, and that all of this planting and thinking and being thankful is just a big hoax and a waste of your time.

Doubts can cripple your efforts and render ineffective your best intentions of planting thoughts. Doubt serves to deflate your dreams and endeavors to make you feel small, insignificant, unworthy, and embarrassed for trying to better yourself and climb out of the pits of despair. Doubts work at the heart of who you are, and as such have unfettered access to your innermost thoughts. That is where they do their most damage, trying to thwart every good thought before it is even launched on its path that will lead to ultimate reality.

When doubt succeeds - you fail! I know this happens because it has happened to me - that's why you have to regularly weed the garden and remain vigilant.

So how do you weed the garden of your mind? How do you stop the doubts, the negative thoughts, and the discouraging moments that seem to always occur without fail at the single-most inopportune time? It may seem to you like you have been broadcasting a message to the universe - "I am at my most vulnerable time - come and get me now"!

So what is doubt and where does it come from? Doubt is described as:

> "... a status **between** belief and disbelief. Doubt brings into question some notion of a **perceived reality**, and may involve **delaying or rejecting relevant action** out of concerns for mistakes or faults or appropriateness. Some definitions of doubt emphasize the state in which the **mind remains suspended between two contradictory propositions and unable to assent to either of them** ..." (emphasis mine)[7]

As for where doubt comes from, it is your ego that requires faith, for your spirit has no problem believing God since God is spirit and - in your essence - you are spirit too. You emanate from the same fabric as God; but as Hebrews 12:9 (KJV) says, He is the "... Father of spirits ... "

Ego must be convinced that God can do what He says, and once convinced, ego realizes that another has taken his place and he is being edged out and no longer depended upon to do what God has promised HE will do - a big bruise to the ego.

Ego is therefore also the source of all doubt, for it is ego in its pride that says "God will not do that for you - just as it's always been - you must depend upon me to do that for you" - and thus doubts arise - just what ego wants - indecision between belief and disbelief in what God has said He WILL do.

Only you can put a stop to it - so you have a choice to make. You can give in to ego's demands, cower in the corner, live in doubt, and let the "weed" of doubt choke your newly planted thoughts to the point of death; or you can stand up to your ego, put it in it's place, proudly and victoriously declare your intention to live by the Law of Attraction, and watch as your thoughts become reality in spite of ego's best efforts to the contrary.

Listen to the words of U.S. Andersen in his book "Three Magic Words":

> "We attract into our lives the physical
> manifestations of the thoughts we think,
> and in order to attract good instead of evil
> we must learn to control our thinking, to
> think positively instead of negatively".[3]

In the silence of your own heart you must learn to master your thoughts and each of you will do it in a different and unique way. For it is there, in your personal holy and sacred place where you and you alone live, that all decisions about how your life will unfold originate. It is there that the still small voice of your will and your conscience reason with you relentlessly. It is there that your ego pleads its case to be the master of your will, and you its slave. It is there that thoughts about your hopes, dreams, and heart's true desires reside in words never spoken to human ears. It is also there that your ego must die if you are serious about making those hopes and dreams reality by successfully deploying the Law of Attraction into your life. You need to plan a funeral and make sure the grave is deep. You need to dethrone your ego and assume your rightful role as master of your life.

Remember the poem entitled "Don't Quit" that I quoted in Chapter 3? One of my favorite parts has some most encouraging lines for all which state:

> "Success is failure turned inside out -
> The silver tint of the clouds of doubt"

You can turn failure into success and protect your planted thoughts from the weeds that would choke and kill them by ridding your mind of doubt and its cancerous thoughts. Be the master of your thoughts - don't let them master you!

As U.S. Andersen observes:

> "Until you become master of your thinking, you will never become master of your fate."[3]

Making Room for the Bounty

One of the fun and exciting things and most anticipated about planting anything is making room for what you are about to receive. Seasonal gardeners take this time to get their canning jars ready, clear adequate space in the storage pantry, purchase all of the needed supplies, and enlist any help that may be required. Farmers prepare their storage bins, check their barns to assure they are in readiness, and get their heavy equipment ready knowing that very shortly they will be inundated with the bounty of the harvest.

For you, thinking through just exactly what is on its way, how it will manifest into your life, and the impact it will have will fill hours of your time with great joy and feelings of satisfaction. This is what you have waited for, what you have planned and executed this process for, your first steps toward a new life created according to your wishes alone. Enjoy the time. Enjoy the feelings. Get excited because your life is about to change! Your harvest is on its way! Preparations must be made!

Carefully thinking through just exactly what preparations you will be required to complete before receiving your bounty - whatever that is for you - may be as daunting a task as planting thoughts has been. Depending upon what thoughts you have planted, the preparations may even require some life changes. Putting money into a bank account is simple, preparing your children for a possible move for a career change may not be as easy.

The central thought to keep in mind is to not allow negative thoughts to creep in since that will hinder, or may even delay the process. If you have thoroughly evaluated the thoughts you have planted using the Law of Attraction, and they are right for you, then this time is what you have worked hard to achieve. These are your dreams about to materialize in front of your eyes and wrapping your mind around actually receiving them will be a brand new experience.

I will close this chapter by relating a personal experience with my thought planting that very well illustrates this point. In Chapter 3 I gave an illustration of how I think from the end about a boat trip I intend to take next summer. I am using the Law of Attraction to obtain the boat for the trip and to transition from my engineering career to my writing career.

While planting those thoughts and engaging the entire process, including this section on Making Room For The Bounty, I realized that in order to obtain the boat and do all I had planted in thought, that I needed to receive an abundance of money. Now I am not against having lots of money, but I have never had that be my life situation. I am a very conscientious person and the moment I realized that an abundance of money would be involved, I immediately began to feel the burden of responsibility that goes along with that. The first thing that popped into my mind was a bible verse that in essence says that to whom much is given, of them much shall be required. It was fun planning for the boat and the trip, but it has been somewhat sobering to think through all of the rest of it.

And that is all part of it and is necessary. A wise person will meter their thoughts and use this awesome law gradually to their benefit. In business when you are upgrading a product offering that has a fixed customer base that is accustomed to your product line, one of the mandates is "evolutionary, not revolutionary".

Your thoughts will soon become things so make room for the bounty!

It's The Law!

Chapter 5
Obstacles in Your Way

"But God made man only to create through thought. Beyond that, each man chooses his own road."
- U.S. Andersen

As with just about everything worth achieving in life, there will be obstacles to overcome. And I think there is great value in obstacles because they challenge our resolve and dedication to the objective pursued. They also help us assign value, for anything achieved easily is generally valued lightly. To be sure, there will be obstacles strewn in your path as you purpose to live your life by the Law of Attraction. And if an obstacle is successful in diverting your attention, it teaches you something about yourself and gives you a good starting point for improvement.

Obstacle #1 - Your Job

Here's your dilemma. You are just learning about the Law of Attraction and wanting to get deeply involved in planting the right thoughts. You've read about it, pondered it, wondered if it is real and for you, and you finally fully commit yourself with the confidence that a new life is just over the horizon. You have had a life full of that dark cloud following you by unknowingly thinking about and planting the wrong thoughts, and have endured the consequences of wrong thinking. You have finally discovered the way to change all of that for the good and have decided this is for you. You carefully follow the steps outlined and pick a single specific thought to start with to test the waters and learn how this powerful and universal law will work uniquely for you. You want to begin to think from the end, frame the future in terms of the present, and imagine your thought as already a finished certainty and on its way back to you.

Your heart is bursting to get started and then it hits you and you question - "How am I going to properly plant this thought when I have to go to work every day? I can't think about this stuff at work and get my job done. These authors who write all of these books have no other full time job and are free to spend as much time as they want planting and cultivating thoughts. No wonder it works for them".

One of the biggest obstacles you will probably encounter is learning how to successfully plant thoughts, think from the end, and express gratitude, while you are at work. After all, if you are like most people, you are there between forty and sixty hours per week, which is a very significant chunk of your week, and you are concentrating on your job so how are you going to think about anything else? When you first get started living into the Law of Attraction and really dedicate yourself to the methods and processes that I have outlined, you may find it very frustrating as you try to determine a way to break through that barrier and spend meaningful time planting your thoughts. But just like everything worth having, you will find a way to make it work.

We all have 168 hours in a week, and if you are average, you will probably spend 56 hours per week sleeping, 55 hours per week commuting to and from work and working, 10 hours per week getting ready for work, and 12 hours per week in food preparation and eating. That leaves 35 hours of free time, most of which is on the weekends or your off days from work. Of that 35 hours, an average of 15 hours are spent watching TV or on other entertainment. Factor in school activities, church, social clubs, sports, family activities, and it is easy to see there is little time left for you to plant your thoughts, think from the end, and express gratitude.

I am just like most of you, hold a full-time job, and work as an engineer five days per week. One way to maximize my time that I have found works well for me is turning off the radio, putting my cell phone on vibrate, and using my drive time - both to and from work - to quiet my mind, organize my priorities, focus my thoughts, meditate, and spend some quality "me" time every day. I so look forward to this sacred time now that I find myself leaving a little early and purposely going out of my way just so I will have more time. I write out sticky notes as reminders of what thoughts I want to plant for the Law of Attraction, think from the end about, and give thanks for. I actually start the time by listening to about five minutes of a CD by one of my favorite authors on the subject as personal inspiration - usually Dr. Wayne Dyer.

In this way, I have found that genuine opportunities to have an attitude of gratitude present themselves every day and my challenge is to learn to actually be thankful for each of them and verbally express it. I have also found that focusing on that one specific thought I am planting comes easier for me while driving since my sub-conscious mind does the driving for me. And once focused, I am able to actually feel the feelings of the wish fulfilled and think from the end as though it were already reality.

While at work, I also have a couple of small sticky notes stuck to the computer monitor with just a couple of simple key words to remind me when I have a free moment what I want to be thinking about. I have also learned to identify other opportune moments that occur every day that allow me to focus my thoughts on my goal. These include walking time to-and-from meetings, bathroom breaks, and lunch break. You probably have many other opportunities if you just think about it. If you have made a commitment to live by the Law of Attraction, any time you can redeem will help you achieve your goal.

Obstacle #2 - Your Family

Much like your job, you may discover that all of your family obligations and family activities will consume large amounts of your time and challenge your resolve to properly execute the processes of the Law of Attraction. Your family is the single-most important influence in your life - and rightfully so. And you must learn to successfully navigate these unknown waters if you want to achieve your goals. This will be especially true if your spouse or significant other does not share your enthusiasm for making the Law of Attraction their way of life. As discussed earlier, the Law of Attraction already affects every part of their life - they just may not know it.

One thing that living more than six decades provides is perspective, and one important truth I've learned is that balance is best in all things and can usually be achieved if diligently pursued. Striking the correct balance will be unique to each individual family but it must be done with rigor. Your family is too valuable for you to allow dissension, which may never be resolved, to drive a wedge because you are absent when you need to be present.

I have also learned that the excitement and intrigue of newfound truths can be addictive and infectious; and that because you are excited you will want to spend large amounts of time pursuing your new passion. If properly channeled and prioritized, this excitement can actually attract other family members by being a portal to exploration and investigation. By honestly answering skeptical questions and inviting genuine curiosity you may turn dissension into an inquisitive interest.

Conversely, if your spouse or significant other already shares your enthusiasm and is learning along with you as a family project, it is a wonderful opportunity to grow together as a family in the mastery of this great law. What better way to send your children out into the world at the appropriate time than to know that they have mastered manifesting through proper thinking and are able to attract back into their lives the things that will help them achieve a happy and productive life.

Make a plan to honestly evaluate your time usage for a week when at home and faithfully record what you observe. If you are thorough, you will find that there are opportunities when you have blocks of time that you can redirect to this law. You may have to temporarily give up a favorite hobby, a sporting event on television, or a night out with friends to purchase this time, but if you are sincere in your desire, your temporary sacrifice will be well rewarded. You will also soon learn that you feel so good after spending time this way that you will uncover even more time to spend; and what you termed a sacrifice has joyfully become an investment in your future well-being.

I turn shower time, yard work time, daily chore time, shopping time, time spent driving to and from errands, any time spent waiting for anything like in a doctor's office, exercise time, walking, jogging, or running time, time in bed before you fall asleep or while awake before getting up, time spent dressing & getting ready for work for the day, leisure time, and personal quiet time into a time to plant thoughts and complete the process. Be creative and redeem every moment and opportunity that reveals itself. Once you start to practice these things, a number of other unique ways will reveal themselves to you. They **are** there - just search for them.

Having to strive to find regular daily quality times will also force you to focus and make your thoughts specific and brief. Why be verbose when brevity will succeed. "I weigh 185 pounds" will probably yield the same results as "I am physically fit, strong, and at my same perfect weight that I was in high school when playing football and running track in my prime".

Your thought planting doesn't have to be long and drawn out - you are planting thoughts not writing a novel. It would be better to find thirty times each day to spend one minute focusing your mind on your thought and going through the process than taking thirty minutes all at one time. That will also afford you the opportunity to change your thought pattern and mindset and think positively in the event an adverse circumstance has presented itself.

It can also become a means to challenge yourself daily and have fun doing it. Just how many different times, places, and ways can you find to plant thoughts? My assessment is - you'll be pleasantly surprised. Can you sneak in a thought between conversations with the kids? How about sneaking one in while you sit in the car waiting for it to warm up a bit? I bet you could sneak one in while your boss is getting his coffee before the meeting starts! How about the time between when you dial the phone and your party answers? Be creative and look for ways - you WILL find them.

Obstacle #3 - Your Guilt

Guilt is one of the most powerful and overwhelming feelings your mind will ever experience. Guilt is triggered by a sense or feeling of short coming or wrong doing no matter what plane the deed happens to reside on. Guilt is called into action by a conscience whose values have been violated, and these violations may be real or imagined. Values normally arise from cultural, religious, moral, or other behavior-dependent belief systems. Prolonged feelings of guilt can have a debilitating effect and result in deep depression. The intensity of the guilt feelings are wholly dependent upon and in direct proportion to the depth and attachment to the belief system that generated them.

Having said that, guilt feelings can also be a type of moral compass that when employed in conjunction with a sensitive conscience help steer your life away from events forbidden by your belief system. Feelings of guilt can range from very slight to extremely intense and thus serve as a crude guidance system.

Parents often times employ guilt to instill moral values into their children. It can be effective if done correctly but may lead to much deeper problems. Guilt can engrave indelible marks on the psyche that may never be erased. The difficulty is, the adverse effect is never usually known until it is too late and the damage has been inflicted.

So how can guilt be an obstacle? Whether we like it or not, most of us carry around a lot of baggage with us - much of it from our childhood and adolescence. How ironic that the time of your life intended to be carefree and invite curiosity and growth often has as its graduation gift an oppressive burden of guilt.

Simply put, your guilt may prevent you from allowing your thoughts to become things - even though they are what you truly want and are within your reach. They are as available to you as to anyone. If appropriating the Law of Attraction positively on your behalf works for any one person, it must work equally for all who apply it. But your guilt may override your best efforts to invoke this law to your benefit and thus frustrate your efforts.

Many have been conditioned to believe that it is wrong to desire to have more than you really need, especially when there are so many people in the world who have nothing. Besides, all those rich people got their money illegitimately and are miserable all the time, as the story goes. But if prosperity and abundance are what you manifest it will not be because you have deprived anyone else of it or taken it from another. Your efforts through the Law of Attraction will be the result of creativity not competition. You are not competing with another, you are creating what you want by attracting it into your life through properly planting thoughts using the Law of Attraction.

Those who have nothing or very little are the ones that need to learn how to use this law properly the most, for they have probably been using this law improperly to their hurt and have most likely been in ignorance about it. And my experience has been that many who are in dire poverty will experience the strongest feelings of guilt for they feel they are not worthy of anything good in life. They have been brain washed to believe that they are not good enough, that their lot in life is to suffer want and struggle for even the most basic of life's necessities, that God is somehow cursing them and there is no hope for a better life. And from generation to generation as the cycle of poverty and despair continues, hope fades.

I know somewhat how they feel - for while I have never been homeless or destitute, I went through a period of extended unemployment right after 9/11 when I lost my job and was unemployed for the first time in my life. My wife and I lost our vehicles, lost our home, lost all of our possessions, lost about everything we owned, and ended up divorced. While several shared a similar plight, I was convinced that I had done something very, very wrong and was no longer worthy to have anything. I made bad, emotion-based decisions at the time that lead to even more despair and even worse decisions.

When you are truly down and out you tend to think that no one really cares, that you are all on your own, that you are just a blight on society, and that you are somehow getting what you deserve. Your mind, through guilt, plays tricks on you as you struggle to survive for just one more day. You try to navigate the convoluted maze of government programs only to be told at every encounter that you don't qualify for whatever reason. My ex-wife even coined the phrase "low income lifestyle" to describe our circumstance and it consists of endless attempts to get the help you need, that you have paid taxes for all of your life, and can never seem to obtain. Your guilt consumes you and soon leads to depression, hopelessness, and despair. It is truly a difficult mental cycle to break.

People in this circumstance need to be convinced that they are equal with everyone else on the planet, that they are worthy of all of the best in life, that if it is available to one, it is equally available to all. And the Law of Attraction is the great equalizer that levels the playing field because it requires nothing more than focused thought - something we all have in abundance. Thoughts can't be sold or pandered by others - they are yours alone. No one can charge you for them or put a tax on them. No one can control or direct your thoughts for they reside and exist in the innermost chambers of your heart and soul, safely tucked away from all who would molest them.

Still others have been trained to believe that you should just be happy with whatever comes into your life, that it is ultimately out of your direct control anyhow, and there is no sense trying to change that.

As the great equalizer, the Law of Attraction offers hope to the downtrodden; but guilt must be overcome before that hope can be enjoined. So how do you overcome this type of guilt? Building or restoring your self-esteem and self-worth will gradually replace the guilt as you realize that you are just as worthy as anyone to use this law. You too, as a unique creation of God, are entitled to dream, and it is He who placed that desire within you. The Law of Attraction is a universal law that works in every person's life, and you already possess all of the tools required to invoke it successfully on your behalf.

Self-esteem and self-worth are matters of perspective - how you see yourself in the world - and these two values are not outside of you they reside within your mind alone. They do not exist in the minds of others even though it is common for those who struggle with them to believe that they do. And realizing that they are functions of your own thinking is key to resolving the struggle, for you alone control your thoughts.

This book is not intended to be a means of treating self-esteem or self-worth problems - there are entire medical fields devoted to them. It is meant however to bring an awareness that these problems will contribute to the obstacle of guilt.

Obstacle #4 - Your Ego

I have left this item for last in this section, but without any doubt, ego will be your biggest and most difficult obstacle to overcome in successfully deploying the Law of Attraction. And the simple truth as to why is that your ego will be insulted and dismayed that the real you, your true essence, would even dare consider entrusting your future to anything or anyone other than itself.

In its mind, your ego has always had your back. Your ego sees itself as the champion of your cause, the captain of your team, and the bulwark that steadfastly defends your honor to all comers. It is your ego that truly believes it acts always in your best interest. It genuinely has no concept of its arrogance, its pompousness, its conceit, or its obsession for power and control. To your ego, these things are business as usual, just standard operating procedure. It expects to play the lead in all ventures of your life and is totally unaware of its own split personality.

But in reality, your ego is a self-aggrandizing impostor, a coward that crouches in fear in the shadows, a mask that once removed reveals a pitifully small and insecure charlatan. It feeds off of the human need for belonging and presents itself as the sole source able to satisfy that need. Its lies are legendary, its pretense without equal, and its fraud all-encompassing. It is your mortal enemy and yet it smiles devilishly as it draws ever closer within your inner circle, waiting for the opportunity to pounce and thrust its dagger of pride deep into your heart.

Your ego is a petulant child demanding attention, and it is incensed that you do not recognize it alone as the source of all of your successes, and that it alone has gotten you where you are. It will remind you that it is the Law of Attraction, wrongly applied, that is the father of all your heartache. How could you ever trust such a law to bring the correct result? It alone is the only one capable of knowing and meeting your needs.

Considering another to captain your ship is the ultimate slap in the face to your ego. It sees itself as your faithful sentinel, always on guard. By correctly employing the Law of Attraction you are summarily terminating your ego for cause and rendering it impotent. It has no thought of slipping quietly into the night.

But its demise can be achieved by following a few basic steps. The opposite of ego is essence, and essence is the real you, who you really are at your core, the part of you which lives forever. Just as darkness is merely the absence of light, the way to overcome ego in your life is to live into your essence daily and show up as whom you really are. Let the world see the real you that God created and intended to be here. Those who believe the bible will recognize this as the battle between the spirit and the flesh.

The more you live into your essence, the more your ego will fade just as more light will cause darkness to fade until it is totally gone. Think of it this way. If your ego is controlling eighty percent of the time, your essence is only controlling twenty percent of the time. The goal is to live into your essence one hundred percent of the time which means your ego is not in control at all. For most people that is a practical improbability. But the goal is to get as close as possible and purpose to maintain as high a percentage as you reasonably can.

To routinely achieve that high percentage, you need to first establish an awareness of ego's level of control in your life. That can best be facilitated by learning the subtle differences that define essence and ego, and then honestly evaluating the influence each has in your life. Only then will you be able to effectively undertake a program to right the ship.

Here is a brief matrix of words that compare and contrast the differences between essence and ego.

Ego Words	Essence Words
Fear Based	Trust Based
Contracting	Expanding
Force	Power
Demanding	Inviting
My Way	Best Way
Driving	Leading
From the Head	From the Heart

Endeavoring to stay in your essence daily, notice how often these words or the philosophy that they identify arises in your life.

The key thing to keep in mind is that your essence is derived from God and never dies, while your ego is the product of the union of your soul and your body and therefore dies when your body dies.

The way to overcome your ego is to:

1. Remember who you really are - the real you, the essence God created
2. Purpose every day, several times each day, to be in your essence not in your ego.
3. Ask yourself several times each day - "How am I doing - essence or ego?"
4. Observe others to determine their status and learn what that looks like
5. Learn the words in the matrix and associate a feeling with each one
6. Add more words and make your own personal matrix for daily use

Your ego is a very strong central character in your life and as such is used to being in control and will not give up its position easily. It is a daily struggle and battle you will likely wage the rest of your life, but it is one that you can win - but it starts afresh and anew the next day when your feet hit the floor.

Obstacles have the potential to become your biggest road blocks in successfully employing the Law of

Attraction for good in your life. If left unchecked - they will thwart all of your efforts and nullify the positive you intend to create. It is one of the main reasons that those who have struggled in life have not been able to break out since the matters that are identified have the potential to hold your mind captive to obsessive thoughts - thoughts that are not in your best interest.

In order for these obstacles not to derail your efforts, you must learn to take control of your thoughts. Whether that is by distraction, by sensory stimulation, by projection, or whatever means, find one that works for you and keep it handy. You never know when a thought, remembrance, or life activity is going to trigger these obstacles in your life. Often an innocent activity such as going to the mailbox results in an unexpected downward spiral of mental obsession from which you must be able to quickly recover.

Remember - by continued right thinking you can achieve your dreams and have the life you have always wanted.

It's The Law!

Chapter 6
The Garden of the Universe

"Man has complete freedom of choice in the kind of thoughts he wishes to plant in the garden of the Subconscious Mind."
- U.S. Andersen

So, where are all of these thoughts actually being planted? That's a very necessary question to have answered since where you plant your thoughts is just as important as how you plant your thoughts. Farmers and gardeners alike will tell you that if the soil you choose for planting your seed is not good soil, all of your fertilizing, weeding, watering, and nurturing will be for naught - proper soil is foundational to the maintained growth of anything planted.

Consistently throughout this book I have referred to the place where your thoughts will be planted as the universe. That's a very nebulous term for an infinitely large expanse to be sure. With that description of your planting field, your thoughts could end up billions of light years away. But I have some place a little more local in mind - actually right in your neighborhood.

I have been purposely vague about this, using the same term as most other popular writers on the subject; but in reality, everything you want or need will come from right here on our planet. No one is shipping things in from Jupiter, or the Andromeda Galaxy for their use that I am aware of.

In this chapter I will get very specific, because your understanding of where you plant your thoughts is mandatory if you desire to experience success with using the Law of Attraction. It is just as crucial to your success as it is to the farmer or the gardener. It is equally possible to plant your thoughts in the wrong place where they will flounder and yield nothing. And you don't want to get this far in your understanding of this promising law and fail because you plant your thoughts in the wrong place. At the end of this chapter you will know specifically where you are planting your thoughts and if it is in-fact the correct place.

What if I were to tell you that there is a perfect soil available; one that needs little or no water, needs no fertilizer, one where weeds will likely not grow, and a soil that guarantees *everything* you plant will not only grow but thrive, and will produce bountifully. Impossible you say? Read on!

In order for you to completely understand where successful thoughts must be planted, some pivotal and crucial groundwork must first be laid. This chapter will require you to think, and at times to think deeply, so it will be best if you can read it undisturbed. It may well expose you to subject matter that you have never explored before; but the importance of your complete comprehension can not be overstated if you aspire to make the Law of Attraction your way of life.

Body, Soul, and Spirit

I want to start by introducing three terms into our discussion with which you are very likely already familiar. You may not have a total understanding of each and how they interface and interact, but all three will occupy an important place in your understanding of where the good soil is.

The three terms are body, soul, and spirit, and in addition to their common usage, these are also biblical terms which are used to define men and women as tripartite beings. In other words, every person who has ever lived possesses body, soul, and spirit. They are separate, significant, unique, and distinct. They exist together in unity and harmony, and contribute equally to your awareness of your existence and standing in different planes of consciousness. That may sound like just so much psycho-babble or some type of new age mysticism but be assured that it is not; and it is imperative that you fully understand the concept presented in the last statement before proceeding further. Since these are primarily spiritual concepts, it will be advantageous to introduce spiritual truths to aid your understanding.

The Body

Presumably you understand what your body is - at least in-part. It is the physical part of you that is made of matter and will one day die. It is the vessel that houses your soul and spirit and the vehicle that moves you around on the planet. Your body is equipped with five senses with which it serves as your gateway to the universe. It is born into this world through the act of procreation; and through a continual growth process, it transitions from infancy, to childhood, to adolescence, and to adulthood before death occurs.

Medical science will tell you that your body is in a constant state of flux through cell replacement, and you never have the same body two days in a row. Your body is unique in all the world and solely yours. It is equipped with a self-preservation instinct and has the capacity to heal itself. While the animal kingdom has a multitude of varying specimens of life, none share completely all of the attributes and complexities of the human body.

Soul and Spirit

Soul and spirit have often been mistakenly identified as the same entity with the terms freely used interchangeably in conversation and literature. Nothing could be further from the truth. In my years of experience with God, I have learned that He is not verbose. He never uses words just to increase His word count, and in I Thessalonians 5:23 (KJV) it very clearly says

> "… and I pray God your whole spirit and soul and body be preserved blameless unto the coming of our Lord Jesus Christ."

The Greek language in which the New Testament was written has two separate and distinct words that are translated spirit and soul in that verse, and every version or translation of the bible that I am aware of includes both. The Greek word pneuma is translated spirit and the Greek word psuche is translated soul.

Pneuma is also translated as breath several other places which is significant since the first mention of man as a tripartite being occurs in Genesis 2:7 (KJV) which records God's creation of man. The verse says:

> "And the LORD God formed man of the
> dust of the ground (his body), and
> breathed into his nostrils the breath of life
> (his spirit) and man became a living soul
> (his soul) (emphasis mine)."

It is clear that the combining of the spirit and the body produced the soul. Thus children are said to be medically "born alive" when the breath of life enters their body and the combining of the two produces a living soul and they begin their conscious life - often with a smack on the rump to start their breathing. This condition is recognized universally.

I was amazed while in training to obtain my pilot's license to learn that when I filed a flight plan usually the last question the flight service attendant asked was "How many souls on board"? That was done in case of a crash to determine the number of living people onboard the aircraft that departed. Air ambulances or other similar charter flights often transport corpses from state-to-state, and in this way if a crash occurred, the authorities were able to determine how many had actually died as a result of the crash.

The Soul

Soul is your conscious mind - that part of you that thinks, that speaks and sings, that observes, that senses, that processes all of your feelings, that reasons, that negotiates the satisfaction of the needs of your body, that contains your personality, that outwardly communicates with its surroundings and by extension, the universe. It skillfully enlists and directs all the functionality of the body to carry out its directives and desires. It grows chronologically in capacity and performance from infancy through adulthood.

It uses the brain as its organ of operation and command center. It is referred to in conversation, literature, and the bible as the heart of man as in "broken heart". It is the seat of your ego. It is the part of you that conceives of wrong doing and occasionally commands your body to perform wrong acts.

Ezekiel 18:4 (KJV) records:

"... the soul that sinneth, it shall die."

Again in Matthew 15:19 (KJV) Jesus said:

"For out of the heart proceed evil thoughts…"

Again in Jeremiah 17:9 (KJV) -

"The heart is deceitful above all things and desperately wicked, who can know it?"

It is your soul where your hopes, dreams, and fears reside. It is your soul that falls in love and seeks that perfect match - a soul mate. It is your soul that is reading this book and endeavoring to learn how to successfully appropriate the Law of Attraction. It is your soul that initiates desires that find embodiment in thoughts that you then choose to plant for action by this law. It is your soul that you must learn to control in your attempts to plant only the correct thoughts for the Law of Attraction.

So the functionality, identity, and areas of responsibility of the soul are well defined and easily documented. I am sure that as you read through that list you could identify with the nature of your soul.

The Spirit

You are not *a* spirit - you *are* spirit - and there is a big difference. Spirit is your subconscious mind and you probably don't know much about your subconscious mind because most people pay very little attention to it. They are too busy and interested in their soul because it is expressive of all of their desires and busy fulfilling the needs of their body; but spirit is the dominant one of the two.

While the soul, or your conscious mind, communicates with your body, the spirit, which is your subconscious mind, is the part of you that never dies and continuously communicates with God who is within you. It is the essence of who you really are, and part and parcel the very same as God.

John 4:24 (KJV) says:

> "God is Spirit, and they that worship him must worship him in spirit and truth".

Hebrews 12:9 (KJV) also calls God:

> "... the Father of spirits ... "

Your spirit is a small fragment of God and he has placed a small fragment within every person born into this world which provides for a direct line of communication with Him. When God communicates with you He does it through your spirit which is your subconscious mind. Consequently, your spirit, or subconscious mind, does no wrong since it is part of God.

Paul records in Romans 7:20 (CEB)

> "But if I do the very thing that I don't want to do, then I'm not the one doing it anymore, instead it is sin that lives in me that is doing it".

As the essence of who you really are, your spirit battles your ego relentlessly for control of your body. When it wins, the real you, your essence, shines forth to all of mankind manifesting forth the kindness, the love, the grace, the mercy, the tolerance, the patience, the beauty, and the abundance of God who is its source of all. Owing to your spirit's continual communication with God, it is also the center of all inspiration in your life.

Your subconscious mind is the part of you that dreams while your conscious mind is asleep. Your subconscious mind actually carries out up to 95% of everything that you do daily. It is programmed by your conscious mind and then it takes over; and that programming occurs by sheer and relentless repetition.

For example, it is your subconscious mind that drives your car every day. There was a time when you were first learning to drive that your conscious mind had to actually learn the steps of driving a vehicle. Once that was mastered, your conscious mind passed it on to your subconscious mind via continuous repetition and now your subconscious mind performs the task flawlessly every time - and it never forgets. You can get in your car, start the engine, put it in gear, drive your same route to work on your daily commute, pull in the parking lot, turn the engine off, exit the car and never consciously think about driving to work. All of those decisions are automatically made for you. You speed up, slow down, make turns, apply the brakes, watch the traffic, and check the mirrors - all without consciously thinking about it. We have all heard the saying "It's like riding a bicycle - you never forget". Anything that is passed into your subconscious mind successfully is there for good, no matter how long the gap between uses.

I am an inactive HAM radio operator and one of the skills I mastered many years ago that, at the time, was a required competency for licensure was Morse code. I could send and receive at a level of twenty words per minute and once you get used to it, it is very much like another language. It has been more than twenty-five years since I learned it and to this day if I walk into a room of a friend who has a radio on in the background and Morse code is being received, I can still "copy" the words in my mind just like the time had never passed. It is in my subconscious mind and will never leave and functions flawlessly every time even if I really don't want it to.

Your subconscious mind is the seat of all habits. Many things you do are the result of your conscious mind having taught your subconscious mind the skills you needed and it in turn made them habits and stored them away for use on demand. Here is just a small list of work, personal, and common habits that your subconscious mind carries out daily with complete perfection at your command:

Work Habits	Personal Habits	Common Habits
Typing	Shaving	Most cooking
Repetitive tasks	Brushing your teeth	House cleaning
Data entry	Combing your hair	Driving
Keypad entry	Tying a neck tie	Walking / running
Writing	Tying your shoes	Climbing stairs
Math functions	Showering	Eating
		Playing piano

Some habits being dutifully carried out by your subconscious mind may from time to time require input from your conscious mind. When that occurs, your subconscious mind pauses its action and awaits further instructions before proceeding to successfully accomplish its task. Once that new piece of information is processed, it is stored for future use should an identical situation arise.

As an example consider using a copier at work. You walk to the copier, automatically place the sheets to be copied into the proper location - all without consciously thinking about it. Since the number of copies is a variable, your subconscious mind pauses while your conscious mind determines how many copies are needed. Once that is done, your subconscious mind resumes control and enters the number, verifies that all other settings are correct, pushes the start button, watches them as they are completed in the tray, picks them up and you then return to your desk. That is why it is possible to carry on a conversation at the same time you are doing all of that because the conversation occurs in your conscious mind while operating the copier occurs in your subconscious mind.

Habits will be discussed again in a different role at the conclusion of this chapter.

It is the express function and responsibility of the subconscious mind to bring into reality what your conscious mind has programmed and identified as what you truly believe. When you hop in your car and your conscious mind relays the need to "drive the car" your subconscious mind then reacts to that and brings to reality your ability to drive the car pausing occasionally if further input from the conscious mind is needed.

None of us who are over the age of three even think about how to walk, yet we get up and walk many times every day. Our conscious mind tells our subconscious mind to bring into reality the ability to walk and it flawlessly recalls its programming and performs the task - directing each muscle correctly in its proper sequence until we arrive at our destination and quit walking.

It's the same with typing, swimming, running - anything that your conscious mind had to learn first. It then turns that task over to the subconscious mind and summons it into reality whenever needed. Athletes are a great example of this process. They go through rigorous training, repeating over and over the actions they desire to master, until these actions and reactions are successfully passed to the subconscious mind for later retrieval. Professional athletes especially excel at this and become very proficient in their trade, many of them earning large salaries for their perfected skills.

As an example, consider quarterbacks in the NFL. Men like John Elway and Brett Favre are prime examples of this process honed to a razor sharp edge. They earned multiple millions of dollars per year for what they were able to train their body to do in short bursts of less than four seconds on average. That is about how much time they had to receive the snap of the football from the center until they had to get rid of it in some fashion; and it was the "some fashion" that separated them, and several others at their same level, from the average quarterback.

The two I mentioned were relentless in their study of the game and fastidious in their mental and physical preparation. They jammed every conceivable scenario that could possibly result from any given offensive play repeatedly into their conscious mind, rehearsing them to the point of physical exhaustion and mental fatigue. The flood tide of conscious thoughts took root in their subconscious mind and on game day the outcome was like a well-played concert, like watching an artist at work, like watching an ice skater perform a flawless, flowing routine.

Play after play they demonstrated their mastery of their craft as four second bursts zipped by. To the uninitiated, they made it all look so easy. But in reality, their subconscious mind was whirring about and had been deftly programmed to respond to every conceivable situation so that their decisions, timed in nanoseconds, were not those of someone mulling a situation over for the first time wondering what they should do next. They had paid forward such a vast storehouse of knowledge against the day of usage that nothing was left undone or wanting.

Another very interesting characteristic of the subconscious mind is that it also responds to mere suggestions from the conscious mind and turns those suggestions into reality. When a person undergoes hypnosis, suggestions are placed into their subconscious mind and it is immediately turned into reality. We have all seen people under hypnosis on television shows that are given silly suggestions such as clucking like a chicken every time a certain stimulus is received. We laugh out loud as they later hear a bell ring and begin clucking!

Other studies in hypnosis to determine the extent of compliance with hypnotic suggestion to the subconscious mind had one person given the suggestion that all of the chairs in a doctor's office were already occupied. When the subject awoke and entered the doctor's office, there were several people in the waiting room but several empty chairs also. The subject stood along the wall fully believing that all of the chairs were already taken. He didn't even see the empty chairs because his subconscious mind told him they were not there. At one point while walking through the office he actually tripped on an empty chair, not recognizing that it was even there.

Having now laid some groundwork and before we move on to the next section, let's summarize what we just learned so that it is fresh in your mind as you approach the next section which is where you will learn about the correct place to plant your thoughts.

- Men and women are tripartite beings.
- Every person born possesses a body, a soul, and a spirit.
- Your body is made of matter and is your physical presence in this world.
- Your body is temporary and will experience death.
- Your body houses your soul and your spirit.
- Your soul is your conscious mind.
- Your conscious mind is the part of you that relates to your physical world.
- Your conscious mind uses your brain as its center of operation.

- Your conscious mind is the seat of your ego - who you want people to think you are.
- Your spirit is a small fragment of an infinite God who is the Father of spirits.
- Your spirit is the part of you that never dies and communicates with God.
- Your spirit is the true essence of who you really are.
- Your spirit is your subconscious mind.
- Your conscious mind programs your subconscious mind with what you truly believe.
- Your subconscious mind brings into reality everything that has been programmed.

The Garden of Your Subconscious Mind

Our logical conclusion then is that your subconscious mind is the garden spot of choice where your thoughts need to be planted for processing by the Law of Attraction. They need to be successfully transmitted from your conscious mind to your subconscious mind where they can be acted upon and brought into reality by this law.

In his book "Three Magic Words", U.S. Andersen has observed:

> "For the Subconscious Mind is a garden, and like the garden of earth that knows only to cause things to grow, the garden of the Subconscious Mind knows only to create reality from the seed of thought. Whether this thought is moral or immoral, ethical or unethical has nothing whatever to do with the inexorable process involved. For the seed having been planted must grow, and grow it will, into physical fact, unless the seed itself is uprooted and another planted in its stead".3

All of the examples about the workings of the subconscious mind given above involve muscle sequencing and data gathering via your five senses, which are already present within your body. So what happens when your subconscious mind is tasked to bring into reality a thought successfully planted by your conscious mind that involves things outside the confines of your body? Your subconscious mind then allies with God, the Universal Subconscious Mind of which it is an integral part, to bring into reality anything it lacks or does not currently possess.

And this is where the majority of your thoughts will likely center - on things you do not currently possess. As each of you seeks to better yourself and improve your life, your need to grow, to expand and express yourself will heighten and you will need tools to accomplish that. These will require your subconscious mind to summon the infinite power of the Universal Subconscious Mind to bring them into existence and retrieve them for you. And the Universal Subconscious Mind delights in accommodating your growth, just as parents delight in the growth of their children. One of the basic tenets of life is growth, and fostering that growth brings real joy.

God, who is the Universal Subconscious Mind and Father of Spirits, in alliance with your subconscious mind or spirit then works to bring all of the people and circumstances together to materialize the thoughts you have planted. That usually takes some time, but whatever is needed is provided. This is the process that takes thoughts and renders them as things in your reality.

So the question then becomes, how do you make sure that the thoughts that you sincerely want to plant for the Law of Attraction get successfully transmitted from your conscious mind to your subconscious mind? I thought you'd never ask!

Transferring Thoughts to
Your Subconscious Mind

Endless Repetition

Identified above is one of the key processes involved - repetition - which is why you need to continue to daily hold the thoughts you plant. Just as you would have to teach your subconscious mind all of the fine details involved in playing a musical instrument, it is the endless repetition that seals the deal. The old adage "practice makes perfect" really is true when it comes to this process.

Studies have shown that for the average person, it takes seven-fold repetition to assure that something is permanently fixed in your mind. And the more complex the subject matter the more repetition is required. That is why you don't learn to drive competently the first time you try - it takes a combination of your muscles and senses interacting repeatedly and your mind storing that new knowledge along with the associated sensations to master the skill. An interesting corollary to this is that if you associate specific feelings and involve as many senses as possible for each thought, the repetition is lessened.

Repetition can at times be quite boring but it serves a very important function. It verifies the credence of the thought to your subconscious mind and fully identifies even the minutest of details associated with it. In order for your subconscious mind to perform flawlessly and render a perfect experience, it has to acquaint itself with the smallest details so that nothing is missing. The only way that occurs is with prolonged repetition.

Genuine Visualization

The subconscious mind makes no distinction between visualizations and real-life situations. As an example of that, think of what happens when you attend a movie, specifically an IMAX movie. You will notice that your heart races, your respiration rate increases, and your stomach reacts to those scenes of being in a plane swooping over the terrain at a low altitude and making all kinds of turns? Your subconscious mind cannot distinguish between reality and images of reality, and thus it causes your body to react as if you were really experiencing the images that are being received by your eyes.

Moviemakers and theaters in general have known that for centuries and have used it to their advantage. That is why the formula for a successful movie or play is not brain surgery. All that is required is lots of action, periods of suspense and drama, scenes that generate sincere and intense emotion, an injustice that must be righted or a cause for which you would sacrifice your life and you probably have a hit on your hands. A movie or play is judged to be a success if it moves its patrons toward real feelings. For it is then that the subconscious mind takes over and forges an experience that is deemed to be real and you react accordingly. If it is a tear jerker - you cry, if it is a wrong that finally gets righted - you clap and cheer, if it is a tale of terror and abuse - you go home and hug your kids and tell them you love them. Your subconscious mind has performed its job to perfection and you feel as though you have actually lived through the experience.

I will never forget when I first saw the movie "Titanic" in February of 1998. It was so real that it haunted me for months to come. And that is what visualization will do, it will cause your subconscious mind to respond as if it were a real situation, and the associated feelings may well linger for a long time, because to your mind it was real - very real. And that is what you are striving for in assuring that your subconscious mind receives the thoughts that you are planting.

With today's technology and the advent of virtual reality, there is no limit to the number of things to which you can expose your subconscious mind. You can be flying the space shuttle today, feeling the vibration and extreme G forces at lift off, and descending into the depths of the Mariana Trench - the deepest place in the ocean - tomorrow, and seeing creatures that have never before been seen by human eyes. If you want to get really adventurous, you can play nine holes at Pebble Beach in the morning, ascend the Matter Horn in the afternoon, tour The Louvre in Paris and dine at Le Meurice when you are finished before jetting back home in your private jet - you are the pilot of course.

All of this is very significant since in Chapter 3 we introduced the need to "think from the end" and visualize your thought as already having been completed. This is the reason for that requirement - because the subconscious mind makes no distinction. And when you truly visualize and feel the associated feelings with your particular thought, you are saying to your subconscious mind **this is real** and it is then programmed to respond and bring your thought into reality no matter what that entails. You have to actually believe it has happened before it does, which is by definition - faith.

Hebrews 11:1 (KJV) states:

"Now faith is the substance of things hoped for, the evidence of things not seen".

Mark 9:23 (KJV) reminds us:

"... all things are possible to him that believeth."

This then is when thoughts become things! And it should demonstrate that it is not difficult to make them a reality. If you're genuine reaction to a movie can cause your subconscious mind to spring into action, then you already have the formula to make the transfer from conscious to subconscious mind. The process is simple. Genuine feelings must be generated within your body, through the use of your muscles and senses, which are then married to specific thoughts that serve to consummate the transaction. Once this is done your reality is on its way to you - just as you conceived of it in your thoughts.

The Here and Now

Your conscious mind has the capacity to think and plan ahead into the future. It is where your dreams originate. The subconscious mind however, functions only in the present - the here and now. Once a thought has been successfully passed to the subconscious mind, it acts affirmatively to bring all the players together and cause the thought to become reality. If the fulfillment of the thought involves skills or other things already in its possession, it responds immediately and creates the fulfillment of the thought instantly - such as riding a motorcycle or playing tennis.

If on the other hand the thought involves obtaining things not in its immediate possession, in alliance with God, it instantly begins the procurement process which then follows the Laws of the Harvest explained in Chapter 2 for fulfillment.

Formation of Habits

Where do habits come from? Most people have habits but never concern themselves with how they showed up in their life, and thus consider them to be externally controlled. From a young age you are told about habits and once defined, you readily recognize their existence within you. To me habits have always been little subroutines in your overall behavior pattern.

Habits are formed by the deepening of thought and behavioral patterns to the point where they become your default for any given circumstance. They are the product of what your conscious mind has been feeding your subconscious mind to the point of saturation. And as we all know, habits can be good or bad, and once entrenched they are hard to change. But this also provides predictability, which can be used to your advantage.

Wouldn't it be great if there were a way to make sure that a great percentage of all of your thoughts were correct thoughts so that you would rarely attract the wrong things into your life? Well there is a way and it is by taking total control of your habits and making your correct thinking a result of habit rather than chance

Habits are one of the easiest and best ways to assure that your life is what you desire it to be. By purposely creating your habits, rather than just allowing them to show up on their own, you can control most parts of your life that in the past have been left to chance or the whim of the moment. Remember, you are transferring thoughts from your conscious mind to your subconscious mind, and the goal here is to make habits of those things that control your thoughts. By doing so, you assure that your thoughts will always be in the correct channels to begin with.

Here are some suggestions for habits to purposely form. These then will become your default reaction.

A Positive Outlook -

How do you react to everyday situations that occur in your life? The weather is rainy instead of the sunshine that was forecast - how do you react? You have a flat tire on a dark country road on a snowy night - how do you react? Your reactions will be in accordance with the habits you have formed and there are only two choices - positively or negatively. Negative reactions are the result of a bad habit being formed, and result in you being upset and antagonistic, neither of which will serve you well. Positive reactions are the result of a good habit being formed and will result in an upbeat, level headed approach to any adversity.

Breaking this habit is not easy but it can be done, and I know because I have personally done it. The key is to stop before you react and make yourself think through it in a positive way. You must control the situation and not allow it to control you. You are at choice for how you react, so start a new habit and begin to react positively by taking a couple of deep breaths and relaxing. Think of positives about the circumstance - they do exist.

I recently had a flat tire on a dark night on an interstate highway after a full day at work, a three hour commute, and only getting three hours sleep the previous night. I was tired, exhausted, and hungry. My recently formed new habit kicked in. Instead of reacting negatively, I began to think of all the positives I could imagine. It was a rear tire instead of front tire so no loss of control. It was on the driver's side - so much easier to get to for changing. It was late evening so the traffic was lighter than it would have been an hour earlier. A friend was waiting to meet me for dinner just three miles away and he came to help me change the tire. I had not checked the spare or jack since buying the ten year old car, but it was all there in great condition. I didn't have a flash light, but my friend's headlights gave us all the light we needed.

When you exchange negative reactions for positive ones, the result is that the positive/negative balance in your daily life swings toward the positive in a significant manner and you just feel happier. When you feel happier, your good habit is further cemented into your subconscious mind and becomes your default. The change will prove to have a drastic impact on your life.

An Attitude of Gratitude -

Complaining about everything that comes your way has become a national pass time. It has been said that complaints are nothing more than a veiled request - a request that the complainer doesn't have the fortitude to make. So instead of trying to correct a situation, it has become easier to just complain. It is a habit that needs to be replaced with the habit of an attitude of gratitude.

Learning to be grateful for everything that comes your way is difficult, but it can be done; and here again, I know because I have personally done it. This was covered in detail in Chapter 3 so I will not go any further here except to say, exchange the habit of complaining with the habit of an attitude of gratitude.

Display Kindness -

Showing kindness is a product of consideration, respect, and understanding - of seeing the best in people rather than the worst, of realizing that we are all equal in God's eyes and intended here by Him. It is easy to find fault and even easier to express your displeasure in others. It becomes a habit that defines you in the eyes of others. Remember, your reputation is not something inside of you, it resides in the mind of others, and it is based on their impressions of you which are gaged by your displayed responses.

Showing kindness as your default position beckoned by habit will require you to extend it blindly, not knowing whether the other person deserves your kindness or not. There are those who genuinely deserve to be shown kindness, and yet others may actually deserve the opposite. But you are not likely in a position to know that, so kindness should be your offering. By giving them what they do not deserve you are extending grace to them, for by definition grace is receiving what you do not deserve. By comparison, mercy is not receiving what you do deserve.

You are at choice for how you treat people, and showing genuine kindness to everyone you encounter will require you to master the ability to look beyond their faults for everyone has them in abundance. It has been said that we easily identify the faults in others that we recognize within ourselves. The phrase used to describe that is "spot it - you got it".

Once again, the habit of finding fault can be exchanged for extending kindness for I have done it and can attest to the positive impact and boost it brings to your life.

Essence Not Ego -

By habit, the vast majority of people live their lives according to the dictates of their ego. Ego was covered in the last chapter and I will not go any further here except to discuss the counterpart to ego which is essence. In the last chapter, ego was identified as one if the obstacles to overcome on your successful path to employing the Law of Attraction in your life. Overcoming that obstacle can be accomplished by exchanging the bad habit of ego with the good habit of essence.

Essence is who you really are, not who you want people to think you are, which is ego. Sometimes the difference is a very subtle shift in the way you think and the way you show up and is evidenced by your attitude. It is easy to be judgmental, critical, and condemning, and most of us received our Master's Degree in that years ago. It is much more difficult to default to finding the goodness in people. That may take some effort while the other is as easy as picking low hanging fruit.

By showing up daily in your essence, you introduce the world to who you really are instead of placing a facade in your place. Ego has been likened to a mask behind which we hide. And I am certain that your experience will confirm that most people act differently at home than they do at work, at church, at social gatherings, at sporting events and other places. You may have thought to yourself, "Wow, what would our company be like if the person he is at work was the same person he is at home with his family?"

You have to work to make showing up daily in your essence your default by habit. And this is yet another bad habit that I have overcome, but this one rears its ugly head occasionally and I have to retrain my subconscious mind for the true habit I want to engage.

In summary, the Law of Attraction states that you attract back into your life what you think about. These thoughts have to be planted correctly and in the proper place for this law to work and in this chapter I have specifically identified where the good soil is and the best way for getting your thoughts planted successfully. As with everything, time to practice and patience will be your friends. But the Laws of the Harvest will work in conjunction with the Law of Attraction as you plant your thoughts in the good soil and great things will happen.

It's The Law!

Chapter 7
The Language of Thought

"I want to know all Gods thoughts;
all the rest are just details."
-Albert Einstein

Because this book is primarily about thoughts, and specifically how they relate to the Law of Attraction, I have included this chapter about the language of thought. That may be a concept that you have never considered, but it is one that is key to fully understanding the Law of Attraction. While I am currently developing this subject into an entire book, I wanted to include some basic precepts here so that you will have a more complete understanding of what thoughts are and how they interact with this law. Most people take thoughts and thinking for granted as a daily function of human life. But there are many layers of complexity concerning the language of thought as you will see.

There are varying theories about thoughts and thinking, and their origin and nature as they relate to the human experience. These theories range from stating that your mind does all of the thinking to your mind does no thinking at all. Trying to categorize and analyze thoughts is a very subjective matter, and the majority of people, if polled, would affirm that they believe their thoughts originate within their mind, at their bidding, or as a result of direct stimulation of their sensory receptors.

The theory that your mind does no thinking at all has been advanced by some very well respected and tenured authors. It is based on the premise that all thoughts originate with God and stream endlessly through your consciousness for your contemplation and review. It further states that you are just a mere observer of these thoughts and elect to accept or reject individual thoughts based upon your choices for life.

Their main argument in defense of this theory is that if you are indeed in control of this endless streaming of thoughts then exhibit your control by causing the stream to stop - totally. Since no one has demonstrated an ability to do that, the conclusion is that you are not the one controlling or originating your thoughts, you are just observing them as they endlessly stream by. Curiously, according to this theory, you can add to and build upon these thoughts, but you do not have the ability to originate thought.

While I greatly respect those who have proposed these theories, and count them among my most revered teachers, I cannot accept this premise primarily because it makes God the author of all of mankind's evil thoughts and that is strictly against His nature. Also, if I am not in control of my thoughts and must wait for the right one to come along, I have a built in excuse for failure and am not responsible since the right thoughts just never came along. If I am not in control of my thoughts, then any attempt at employing the Law of Attraction for good in my life is a futile exercise and doomed to failure.

Now I do believe that God gives you insights, passive leadership, and unspoken direction, all of which show up as thoughts in your consciousness, and all at your bidding. It is not God's nature to force Himself upon anyone. But as you seek to know Him better, He reveals Himself to you more and more. You are an individual expression of the nature and character of God, and as such, your thoughts are your own. How else could expressions of love, gratitude, devotion, or commitment mean anything? If they are merely the thoughts of God being parroted back to God by an automaton, and not genuinely spawned from a sincere heart spontaneously without supreme urging, they lose all meaning.

A favorite professor of mine in college used to espouse a popular idiom to all his students who were struggling to interpret difficult bible verses. His favorite saying was "If common sense makes sense, seek no other sense." My common sense and experience tell me that I originate my thoughts and can cause them to focus on any subject of my choosing at any given moment.

The trend of my thoughts is solely in my discretion, and the fact that I cannot stop them proves nothing about their origin. That would be tantamount to saying that because I cannot stop my heart from beating it is not my heart. The nature of your heart in part is to beat at varying rates until the body dies and the nature of your mind in part is to create thoughts.

The essence of consciousness is first of all self-awareness. We all have a constant ongoing inner dialogue of thoughts playing inside our mind and these are the thoughts that comprise and define the ebb and flow of our daily lives. The controlling of this daily ebb and flow in a manner consistent with your overall life goals is the purpose of this book.

Most of the time, your thoughts are being guided by current ongoing input from your five senses. For example, think of driving your children to school in the morning; what are your thoughts centered on? As you back out of the driveway you are thinking about the possibility of traffic on your street and making sure you back out safely. Your thoughts swiftly change to the argument escalating in the back seat as your ten year old son decides it is a perfect time to tell your eight year old son what a stupid jerk he is. Not to be left out, your twelve year old daughter declares that they are both jerks and a major embarrassment to her when her BFF Julia comes to visit. By now you are stopped at the corner waiting for the traffic light to change when you notice the beautiful pink clouds that form the tapestry of a beautiful sunrise. For a moment your thoughts travel fifteen hundred miles and three months into the past to a very similar sunrise on the last day of a romantic weekend away with your husband. Ahhhh how nice that was!!! "Who is that idiot behind me honking his horn - OH the light is green - oops! Jude quit throwing things at your brother - you need to be a good example for him." And on and on it goes. You have all been there - way too many times - and you know it's true.

The vast majority of your thoughts throughout the day are a direct result of what is right in front of your nose - the input of your senses. Your immediate attention is always focused on the present in front of you with one exception. When what is in front of you can be handled by your subconscious mind, your conscious mind passes the responsibility off to your subconscious mind and your conscious mind is then free to think about something of its own choosing.

A good example of that is taking a trip in the car by yourself. You know you have over two hours until you reach your destination and once clear of traffic the car goes on cruise. Your subconscious mind has been driving the car since you left your house and now that you are en route, you have time to listen to a book on audio or whatever you want. Your mind is relaxed and free and you direct its thoughts where you want them to go.

I am not going to develop this thought here more than just to briefly mention it - but your brain is not your mind. Your mind works in close conjunction with your brain, and your brain is the very sophisticated organ that takes your thoughts and translates them into controls for your body. Since your essence is spirit which never dies and your body, including your brain, dies, it is apparent that you brain is not your mind. That is an extremely simplistic stating of a very complex concept to be sure, but it is hopefully enough to whet your appetite.

Thought and Language

What languages do you speak? This book is written in American English and may at some point be translated into other languages. There are hundreds of languages throughout the world and thousands of local dialects. Language, while not the only means of communication, is foundational to most communication.

Language is the formation of individual concepts or thoughts into specific defining words which may or may not be verbalized. If they are verbalized then they are expressed by specific and unique groupings of audible sounds. Once verbalized, these specific groupings or patterns of audible sounds are received by the auditory nerves of the hearer and recognized as a specific word or concept with the identical associated meaning. Thus we have an efficient means of communicating our thoughts and feelings in a structured manner.

There are numerous languages but the underlying thoughts and concepts of each language are similar in structure which facilitates interpretation of these concepts and thoughts between languages. Consequently, when an English speaking person has a concept of gratitude the term "thank you" is generated in their mind. A Spanish speaking person with the same basic concept generates the word "gracias". A Japanese person could generate one of a couple words but would likely generate the word "domo", and an Italian person would generate the word "grazie". But they are all verbalizing an identical concept even though the sounds of the various words are quite different.

But there is another underlying foundational plane of language above the formation of words and it is the language of thought which is also the language of spirit and the language of God. The language of thought is rudimentary, foundational, wordless, and universal. It is a language common to all human life and its true essence and nature I can only best describe as a knowing-feeling-understanding. The bible alludes to it thusly in Romans 8:26 (KJV)

> "And in like manner the Spirit also helpeth our infirmity: for we know not how to pray as we ought; but the Spirit himself maketh intercession for us with **groanings which cannot be uttered**"(emphasis mine)

Those "groanings which cannot be uttered" comprise the wordless, universal, language of thought.

There are times when people are in great pain and despair, usually caused by an unthinkable tragedy, and they literally cannot find words to express the knowing-feeling-understanding that intensely resides within them. It is at times like this that the foundational language of wordless thought communicates itself clearly to God, and He well understands for it is communicated in His own universal language.

This language of thought is present in new born babies and toddlers before they know a spoken language and allows them to communicate their wants and needs without spoken words. Since it is present in all human life, it also allows those born with sensory deficits to communicate at a very basic level with great efficiency. This wordless, universal, language, is the fundamental language of consciousness, and all spoken languages are a subset of this universal language.

We have all experienced situations where we are trying to say something and can't find the exact word that fits precisely. My experience is that this happens more frequently when you are writing as opposed to speaking. Your mind searches your active vocabulary and may find a word that comes close but is not exactly what you want to say. As you mull it over in your mind, that underlying knowing-feeling-understanding is in-fact the language of spirit and thought. It is wordless at that point and consists of what I call a knowing-feeling-understanding and may generate a visual image in your mind. You continue to search your vocabulary until you arrive at the exact word or closest match. It is interesting that there are many times when there are no words in your vocabulary that match the knowing-feeling-understanding that is present in your mind and you have to settle for the next best thing thus leaving your true knowing-feeling-understanding not completely expressed. This happens frequently when we try to express feelings that are deep and abiding like love, devotion, and affection.

You can experience this for yourself and have some fun with it. The next time you find yourself "at a loss for words" savor the moment. Try not to rush forward - just stay in that moment - and invest the time to thoroughly analyze what you are experiencing and do your best to quantify the event. What are your senses telling you, if anything? How would you describe what you are experiencing in your mind? You can actually slow this process and examine it fully with a little practice.

What you are experiencing as you try to find the precise word to express what your mind is fixated on is the language of thought - and it is very real and universal. Every person has that same exact, precise, knowing-feeling-understanding in the inventory of their consciousness, and based upon your predominant spoken language, your mind arrives at the unique word or grouping of words that best describe that knowing-feeling-understanding.

I only speak and write American English fluently, but I have a cursory knowledge of several other languages - as the saying goes, I know enough to get myself in trouble. I know a little about Greek and Hebrew from my Bible College days and subsequent studies. My engineering career has introduced me to just a passing acquaintance with Japanese, Italian, and Spanish. In my exposure to these I have learned that there is a vast difference in the scope, reach, and structure of these different languages.

For example, and this is a very simplistic rendering and not meant to be a study in grammar, the aorist tense in Greek has a meaning which has no equal in English. The aorist tense of a verb defines a past completed action with present results, as opposed to just a past completed action.

Consider this sentence. I married in 1969. In English you have no knowledge of whether the marriage is still in place. If the sentence in Greek used the aorist tense for married it would mean I married in 1969 and am still married today. Do you see the difference?

So if your mind wants to express that knowing-feeling-understanding in English you will have to choose several words instead of just one if you were expressing it in biblical Greek.

Empty Thoughts

What is meant by the term empty thoughts? How can a thought which emanates within your mind ever be considered empty? It is empty if it is not accompanied by the knowing-feeling-understanding that normally originates and generates that specific thought. In that instance, it is a faux copy and lacks its original authority. I say authority because your thoughts carry the authority to command that they be made into things by the Law of Attraction.

All verbalized words are expressed thoughts, and when the thoughts behind them are insincere and are not the product of the knowing-feeling-understanding process that constitutes genuineness, they too are empty and void of any real meaning. We have all experienced occasions when the people speaking to us are rightly perceived as disingenuous. One of the classic examples and the subject of many jokes is a used car salesman as he declares "It was owned by a little old lady who only drove it to church on Sundays." We have all listened to people apologize for a wrong-doing knowing full well that their heart was not in what they were saying.

These empty words are the children of empty thoughts. The thoughts are there or the words would never be spoken; but the knowing-feeling-understanding that legitimately fathers those thoughts is curiously absent. They are meaningless and everyone knows it - even the person who tenders them. They are clouds without water, offering hope and promise that is left unfulfilled.

The Law of Attraction requires genuine thought born of an authentic knowing-feeling-understanding for it to work. These are the thoughts you are passionate about - they are your future in embryonic form and that is a serious matter not to be taken lightly. Many a person has failed with the Law of Attraction and this is why - their thoughts were empty. In the words of the musician - they had no soul. They were just going through the motions, the rituals, in which resides no life or power to cause anything to happen.

Many think that if they flood the universe with their thoughts, they will be certain to affect the change they desire. But vain repetition will also generate empty thoughts. Commanding your mind to develop thoughts for the Law of Attraction and repeating them over-and-over with no emphasis on an undisputed knowing-feeling-understanding will yield nothing but frustration and will get you nowhere. Focusing on quantity over quality will earn you the prize of disappointment.

You have to be real when you approach this law with your thoughts and the reality has to be demonstrated. Your attitude has to be one of authenticity and **every thought** must be born in genuineness. It is easy, with as busy as everyone is today, to try to hurry through and get on to the next thing on your calendar, like you do with many other things in your life. That may work with things like attending PTA meetings or running errands, but the Law of Attraction demands your full attention if it is to yield the outcome that you desire.

One thing that will help you is familiarity with something called Attention Levels. There are three attention levels of our consciousness, and our thoughts continually and seamlessly jump from one to the other all of our waking hours. Notice the graphic below.

S_{elf}	Level 1
O_{thers}	Level 2
S_{urroundings}	Level 3

Attention Level 1 is all about self. This is when you are paying attention exclusively to what is going on inside of you. You may be thinking about your hair style, how your clothes fit, what you are going to say when asked why you were late to work - any number of things. You are internalized and oblivious to anyone or anything else.

Attention Level 2 is all about others. You are focused on a conversation with another person and listening intently. You are not thinking about anything or anyone else except the person with whom you are engaged in conversation. You are making constant eye contact and your focus is solely on that individual.

Attention Level 3 is all about your surroundings. What is going on in the room or environment all about you? You notice things like the spirit of the room if you are in a room full of people. Is it light-hearted, spirited, quiet, or subdued? Level 3 is all about your surroundings.

Now let's notice how you move seamlessly between these three levels all day every day - and all of this is very normal. It will also help you identify areas of weakness that need improvement. Consider the following scenarios.

You are sitting listening to your best friend over coffee as she recounts her recent experience at the doctor's office. You are totally Level 2 and something she says triggers a thought of I need to say this when it's my turn to talk. You just went from Level 2 to Level 1 when thinking of your response instead of focusing on what was being said. After securing your response, you're back in Level 2 listening intently. All of a sudden the sound on the TV located on the wall behind her erupts with raucous cheering. You look away momentarily at the TV screen just in time to see a runner score a touchdown. You just went from Level 2 to Level 3. You refocus on your friend and are back at Level 2. Suddenly you notice that a bee has just landed on her shoulder. You think, "What should I do?" Just at that time before you can say anything, the bee takes off and you refocus on your friend's conversation. You have just gone from Level 2 to Level 3 to Level 1 and back to Level 2. It happens all day every day and is very normal.

The benefit of knowing about these attention levels is that you can determine which one you are currently in and adjust as needed to assure that your thoughts are focused where they need to be. You need to stay in Level 1 with your thoughts for the Law of Attraction and make sure they are sincere and real. They should reflect your true passions for then the feelings will be authentic and never empty. They will be born of the knowing-feeling-understanding that defines the language of thought.

In summation, the Law of Attraction as it applies to your thoughts simply states that you attract back into your life what you think about. And this chapter has endeavored to give you a clearer understanding of the true nature and language of thoughts. Your thoughts are a bridge from your past to your future. What you think about you will become.

It's The Law!

Chapter 8
When Forbidden Fruit Becomes Food For Thought

*"There is a charm about the
forbidden that makes it
unspeakably desirable."*
- Mark Twain

The title to this chapter has its origins in the biblical account of Adam and Eve in the Garden of Eden. It seems that even very early on, God wanted to make sure we all were aware that when you allow your mind to wonder into wrong places, bad things happen.

Many years ago I happened to be visiting Bob Jones University with a good friend of mine. He was a well-known and beloved pastor, had a large church in southern Ohio, and was speaking at a chapel service at the university that day. We had flown down the afternoon before in a plane that I had rented and the university had provided us with accommodations on campus.

As I unpacked some of my things for the night, I happened to see a catalog from the university on a table and leafing through the pages my eyes fell upon some sermon titles by Dr. Bob Jones III that were available on audio cassette (boy that dates me for sure). As I glanced through the list, one in particular caught my attention, "When Forbidden Fruit Becomes Food For Thought". I didn't purchase the cassette, but I never forgot the title - it has haunted me for many years. It made a deep and lasting impression on me because of the simplicity with which it clearly defined a very serious reality of life.

We often speak of various topics as being food for thought - meaning that they are very worthy of a person spending a considerable amount of their time thinking about them. Little did I know that twenty-seven years later I would use that same title as the final chapter of this book. And the reason I am making it the final chapter is because it is impossible to over-emphasize or over-state the potential for utter disaster that awaits those who allow their thoughts to be focused upon forbidden fruit.

I have tried to thoroughly explore all relevant aspects of thought since thoughts ultimately become things, and thus thoughts are the singular currency that when tendered will secure your future - whatever that may look like.

As the Genesis account makes clear, Adam and Eve had been given permission to freely eat of all the things in the garden with the exception of the fruit of one particular tree - the tree of the knowledge of good and evil. But the record reflects that Eve was apparently spending significant time looking at the tree and her assessment was that it was good for food, pleasant to the eyes, and could make her wise.

Isn't that always the way? We are never satisfied with what we have and always want what we can't or shouldn't have. It's not like they were experiencing scarcity, they had all they needed in great abundance - they just allowed themselves to think about the one thing that had been forbidden. And the more they thought, the more they desired, and the more they desired the more they obsessed, and the more they obsessed the more they coveted that which had been forbidden, until at last they could no longer resist and decided that no matter the consequences, they had to have that fruit.

Theirs is a story of uncontrolled thoughts and the ramifications brought about by runaway desire. They had pure abundance but wanted more. The saying "The grass is always greener ..." comes to mind, and for some reason, the allure of always seeking more grabs hold and will not let go.

You can spend hours reading this book, learning exactly how to plant thoughts for the Law of Attraction, spend days, weeks, or even months faithfully and flawlessly executing the prescribed plan and waiting for harvest season to arrive and end up worse off than you were because you allow wrong things to take up residence in your mind and make themselves at home there.

I wrote this book because I genuinely want you to succeed with this amazing Law of Attraction. I want you to find what I have found - that this law will help you have a better life. It will help your kids have a better life. It is a simple plan that just works and it works because it is a universal law. It also works on bad thoughts with the same amazing accuracy and absoluteness as it works on good thoughts. That which you love and swear by when you are thinking right thoughts will quickly become that which you hate and curse when your thoughts are not controlled.

Listen to U.S. Andersen again.

> "Accordingly, there is no more paramount thing for you to do than **carefully** select

those thoughts that you will think, those beliefs you will adopt, those attitudes you will take for your own, *for by them you will be what you will be;* by them you have arrived exactly where you are today. If you mean for your life to be progressive and full of achievement, vigor, love, and abundance, you will abandon each negative thought the moment it is presented to you. You will refuse to accept on the plane of mind any conception other than those that are in tune with good. You will think only positively! And the universe will shower you with more good than you ever dreamed." (emphasis mine)[3]

Thoughts *will* become things - it's the law! And inappropriate thoughts will assuredly become inappropriate things. In this final chapter, I will describe for you several of the major distractions that you will easily recognize as having been occasional food for thought. And depending upon your life circumstance, you may recognize that your mind is already feasting on these all too frequently. You must consider them to be forbidden fruit and not allow your mind to feed on them. At the end of this chapter I have laid out a simple plan to assist you in overcoming these distractions and not allowing forbidden fruit to become food for thought.

Financial Issues

It is amazing how quickly your mind can be moved off of the correct path onto an onerous path that leads to despair and discouragement. Just a simple thought or innocent remembrance has the potential to jettison you from the path for days on end. And your personal finances are one of the areas in which you are the most vulnerable.

Almost everyone has struggled with finances at some point in their life. Even those who are very wealthy wrestle with finances. The scale of their battle is unimaginable to most, but to them, in their particular circumstance, it is still a struggle.

I like to play blackjack and would occasionally indulge myself at a local casino. I always set a very modest loss limit and would faithfully leave the table if and when it was reached. One thing I observed early on was that there were a number of people betting a lot more per hand than I was. They would bet $100 when I was betting $5 and I noticed that when they lost it was no more devastating to them than my $5 loss was to me. If I had lost $100 on a single bet I would have been in cardiac arrest and my loss limit immediately reached. It is a matter of scale. So everyone struggles with finances at some scale – it's just a fact of life.

But financial difficulties have the potential to incapacitate your mind at its very core and underpinning. Their debilitating power is second only to bodily disease or death. They have the ability to cause you to focus on nothing else and wreak havoc with any attempts at peace of mind. The single thought or remembrance soon becomes a constant procession of cascading remembrances that, with ever-increasing intensity, consumes your mind with a steady drum beat. Your mind becomes so focused on resolving the financial struggle that all else is blocked out.

Financial struggles are one of the leading reasons given for divorce today. When couples fall on hard times for whatever reason, the outcome is often the dissolution of the union; and the intense thought process that pervades the entire and many times years long struggle, leads to depression and bitterness, and drives deep a wedge that destroys the once invincible relationship.

Thoughts enter your mind that were not even on the planet when times were good. You soon discover that there is a side of you that, when backed into a corner, responds with thoughts you never dreamed you could have. It is truly amazing the myriad and variety of thoughts and ideas that cross your consciousness. In times like this, sane, moral, law abiding, and peaceful people make uncharacteristic choices that would never enter their mind otherwise. Many turn to criminal activity with its allure of quick, easy cash as a means to relieve the constant mental pressure. You can rationalize almost anything when the wellbeing of young children and other loved ones is at risk.

So just how does the mind work in these extreme and difficult situations? It basically responds by reverting to the *fight or flight* mode that we all possess as a self-preservation mechanism. Your mind, in harmony with your body, has the ability to shut out all else till the problem is resolved. Your mind and body will even begin to curtail activity or shut down bodily systems if it regards the circumstance to be dire enough. Most financial struggles do not meet the criteria of a life or death situation, but your mind and body are programmed with self-preservation as their prime directive.

And if you are in a financial struggle and trying to plant correct thoughts to overcome that struggle, you will have a battle on your hands trying to maintain your focus because you are fighting your own body for control of your thoughts. Intellectually, you know *you* are right, but your body has been programmed with a primal instinct that does not listen to reason, even if it is coming from you.

These financial struggles then must be tagged as forbidden fruit and avoided if you plan to succeed with planting thoughts for the Law of Attraction.

Health Issues

Taking care of your personal health is something you generally do as a matter of habit, and annual checkups have become an integral part of a conscientious health regimen. These annual examinations are also credited as the primary vehicle for early detection of serious health problems, especially in senior citizens. It is perfectly normal then and expected behavior for those diagnosed with a serious illness to spend a reasonable amount of time in thought about their condition and the impact it will ultimately have on their life and the lives of those close to them.

But health issues, especially serious or terminal ones, have the potential to totally occupy your every thought. As someone who has been close to many others who have been terminal, obsessing about your medical condition is probably the worst thing you can do, but probably the most understandable also under the circumstances.

It is normal upon learning of a serious or terminal condition to think through all of the ramifications of the changes that lie ahead. Plans have to be made, unique decisions present themselves, and reality sets in as your world irrevocably transforms before your eyes. Medical professionals will tell you that after the initial onslaught is navigated, successfully getting your thoughts off of your condition is beneficial to both your physical and mental wellbeing. Continued obsessive thought then assumes the role of a forbidden fruit.

Other non-critical or non-life threatening medical issues, once diagnosed and professionally treated, will also tend to occupy your mind and may present problems. Anytime your body is diagnosed with a malady, your self-preservation instinct begins to kick in and your mind begins to obsess about it. If you are trying to plant thoughts for the Law of Attraction, even though you are following the prescribed treatment, the illness will challenge your conscious mind for priority status. That is why it must be labeled as forbidden fruit, since it has the potential to totally obliterate your thought planting efforts.

And to make things worse, if you succeed in getting your mind to focus on the thoughts you are planting with the Law of Attraction, your family members are usually right there to remind you of your health issues by continually bringing it up. I am certain they mean well, but to them, asking you about your health shows their concern for your wellbeing.

It has also been my observation that the older people get the more they talk about their health issues. I am in my mid-sixties and it is an easy conclusion to draw. Owing to the fact that seniors have more serious health issues than any other sector of society, it is certainly normal and expected behavior. But it draws attention to the fact that concentrating on planting thoughts for the Law of Attraction at any age while in the midst of a medical crisis will continue to be a challenge. Thus it rightly earns the label of forbidden fruit.

Relationship Issues

Nothing stirs your emotions, steals your focus, and hijacks your thoughts like matters of the heart. Many define love as an emotion but I disagree and believe it is much more than mere emotion. To me love is a condition of the heart or soul that mandates unselfish commitment - no matter who the recipient is. We are all capable of giving and receiving love, and each time we do, we willingly accept whatever level of commitment is mandated. Love is a very powerful suitor that grabs hold of you and refuses to let go. Your thoughts quickly become its hostage if even the tiniest of problems arise.

We value our human relationships above all else in our life and rightfully so. Even our own health and wellbeing are secondary in importance to our love relationships and these relationships can be with any other person with whom we are very close. Some of the strongest of these are the husband and wife relationship, the fiancée relationship, the significant others' relationship, the parent - child relationship, the sibling relationship, the grand parent - grand child relationship, and the aunt/uncle - niece/nephew relationship. There are many others to be sure, but these form the core of the strongest human relationships.

If you find yourself in the throes of a problem with one of your relationships, you will find it almost impossible to focus your thoughts any place else. And just like your health issues, you certainly need to spend an appropriate amount of time thinking how to proceed with the problem. And just as the medical professional advises the critically ill patient to limit the time he thinks about his condition, relationship counselors and therapists also advise those going through relationship struggles to get their mind off of their problems, also for their physical and mental wellbeing. Being a pastor for twenty five years exposed me to first-hand real-life relationship struggles that verify this as true.

The obsessive nature of your ensuing thoughts will totally negate any attempts you are making at planting thoughts for the Law of Attraction. And perhaps they need to be suspended until the issue is resolved, especially if they are not germane to the relationship. But if the thoughts you are attempting to plant are intended to help your relationship, then these obsessive thoughts must be labeled as forbidden fruit and avoided to the best of your ability, so that proper thoughts can be successfully planted.

We have all been through times when a relationship struggles and we all know how thoughts seem to take on a life of their own, refusing even the most gallant attempts at redirecting them. Your heart is generally breaking and your mind is busy being hurt, angry, scared, frustrated, sympathetic, acquiescing, and many more. And each of these generates a separate scenario for a conversation you intend to have with your loved one. Your thoughts are darting all over the map and you soon become overwhelmed. Trying to plant thoughts for the Law of Attraction in the midst of this quagmire will be a lost cause to be sure.

What Is Natural For You?

This forbidden fruit needs to be fully understood and avoided. The words of Jesus in Matthew 6:27 (KJV) state:

> "Which of you by taking thought can add one cubit unto his stature?"

The obvious truth being presented here is that there are certain things in your life that are not changeable - even by the Law of Attraction, and these things help to define what is natural for you.

The caution here is twofold. Don't let this point discourage you from attempting anything you wish to create using the Law of Attraction; but also know that the efficacy of this law will be bounded by what is natural for you.

I can almost hear people saying "OK, here we go. I knew this was too good to be true. You wait till the last chapter and drop a bomb." I would be remiss if I didn't tell you the whole story, and besides, this is not a negative, it is a positive. It will help you focus your thoughts on things that you can create and not waste time on things that you can't change. And the list of things that comprise what is natural for you is very limited and mostly common sense, but they need to be addressed and identified as forbidden fruit.

These items include such things as your height, your eye color, your skin color, your gender, your foot size, etc. The list will differ for everyone since it is what's natural for *you*. There are medical procedures available to change some of these things, and you can buy contact lenses to temporarily change your eye color, but these items, in my estimation, are not candidates for the Law of Attraction.

Not only the items themselves, but the impact they have due to their nature is also in view here. For example, if the requirements for being an astronaut limit your overall height to a specific number - say six feet tall - don't try to use the Law of Attraction to shrink from your current six feet eight inches tall down to six feet tall. It isn't natural for you and it should be considered forbidden fruit.

When considering what is natural for you be aware that as you age, these things will change. What is natural for you at the age of ten is not the same as what is natural for you at the age of fifteen, or eighteen, or thirty five, or older. Charles Haanel stated in his book "The Master Key System":

"The three things which all mankind desires and which are necessary for his highest expression and complete development are Health, Wealth and Love."[11]

As you go through the aging process, the specifics of what is natural for you concerning health, wealth, and love will change dramatically. And that is because you will change dramatically also.

Carefully consider the thoughts you are planting to assure yourself that they are what is natural for you. But don't make the mistake of thinking that your past dictates what is natural for you.

Think of a boat moving through the water and the wake it leaves behind. The boat is you, always moving forward in your life, and the wake is your past. You can easily see your past as you look backward at the wake and it will tell you where you have been and the right or wrong turns that you made. But the wake of the boat has no influence whatsoever on where you steer the boat next - that is totally up to you as the captain of your life. If you see a storm ahead, you will undoubtedly make a course correction. If you see fair winds and following seas ahead, your course will probably be steady as she goes.

Being an avid boater, this illustration hits the mark and full well describes the relationship between your past and your future. Their only point of interface is the instantaneousness of the here and now - that's it. And the past has absolutely nothing to do with what's coming next for you. Only your thoughts determine your future, and they are what you create them to be.

The way it has always been does not mean it is the way it must always be. Your present condition *is not* your final condition. Your future will be what you make it, and the Law of Attraction is the tool that will get you there.

Program for Overcoming These Mind Traps

A lot of remedies I have read say to just change what you're thinking about. That's not always easy to do - in fact I find it nearly impossible at times. So I set about to identify times in my life when it was occurring and find a solution that goes beyond just changing what I'm thinking and present that program here.

You Are "At Choice" To Think What You Want

One of the things that works for me is to remind myself, sometimes a little harshly, that we are all at choice to center our thoughts on the subject of our choosing. No one can control your thoughts but you, and when you identify circumstances where you want to change your thoughts, make the decision and follow through. Here are a few suggestions for activities that will assist you to "change the channel" of your thoughts.

Flood Your Mind with Input from Your Senses

Your senses are the only means by which you are able to introduce anything into your mind. Everything you have ever placed into your mind since you were born into this world came via your senses. Flooding your mind with sensory input will help you change your thought pattern and break the log jam of obsessive thoughts. When your mind is overly engaged, you will find that you are generally alone and actively seek quiet places of repose to accommodate your excessive thought pattern. Here are a few activities to consider to help flood your senses.

Listen to fast, up tempo, and energetic music!
Music is a medium that touches several senses. Not only do you hear it, but you feel it and often times can see it if there are orchestrated lights associated with it.

Go to an amusement park at night and ride several rides! An amusement park at night is full of sights, sounds, smells, feelings, and tastes, so indulge yourself. There is not a much better place to get all five of them at once.

Go to a casino and look, listen, and eat at the buffet! A casino is another place that virtually explodes with flashing lights, the continuous signature ring of slot machines paying off, plenty of good food and beverages, and plenty to touch with the games. Even if you don't like to play, your senses will be on high alert.

Go to a water park and jump into cold or cool water! Nothing quite matches a water park for pure fun in the sun. The sights and sounds as you hit the wave pool or the gigantic water slides and hear the shouts of excitement from the throng of kids enjoying themselves is impossible to replicate anywhere else. And jumping into cool water on a hot day will bring goose bumps. You will feel something there for sure.

Make love to your spouse! For those who are married and in love, nothing fills the senses like making love and enjoying the company of your spouse. Guess I will stop right there before I get bleeped! You get the picture!

Go to a buffet or smorgasbord and take in all of the succulent aromas before you eat! Enjoying great food will make your senses feel totally alive. Not only do you taste the heavenly recipe, but the combined aromas of the entire offering of a buffet or smorgasbord come close to being overwhelming. The sounds of the food being prepared or served, as in stir fry, serve to heighten the experience. Aren't you glad that humans get to enjoy food and are not like animals that merely eat to survive? How tasty can grass really be anyhow?

Go to a petting zoo and touch as many animals as possible! Touching is one of our greatest senses. It physically connects us to our environment and helps us to realize that God has creatures of all shapes and sizes and He loves them all. We feel the texture and character of the animal that has captured our attention. When you pet animals in a petting zoo, you feel the warmth of their body if they are warm-blooded, feel the blood coursing through their veins, feel the fur or coat that is their natural covering, and usually feel their wet tongue on your hand or arm. You also see the animal respond favorably to your touch and hear them utter their native sounds of approval at your stroking. Most animals have a scent associated with their species that is very unique.

Flooding your senses will prove to be a successful way to break a session of mind lock - where you can't get

your mind off of some forbidden fruit. Use your senses
to your advantage - they are there for a reason.

Distract Your Mind Aggressively

**Watch an action movie in the theater or on
television**. Getting lost in a movie, especially an action
movie or a mystery, is an effective way to change your
thought patterns. It provides a ready-made
environment for your mind to engage in something
totally different for a period of time - and that period of
time will probably be of sufficient length to stop the
excessive wrong thoughts.

Sing several robust and happy songs. Singing is a
wonderful way to change your thoughts and lift your
spirits at the same time; and when you are fixated on
forbidden fruit, both are usually necessary. Singing
involves emotion and introducing yourself to the good
feelings that accompany happy songs will seal the deal.

**Watch a sporting event in person or on
television.** Few things fully engage your mind like
sporting events that you are passionate about. And if
you can actually attend the event, that is even better
because you also get the benefit of all of the usual
trappings of the event, like food and beverages.

Play a musical instrument if you can. If you possess the talent and skill to play a musical instrument, spending time playing through part of your repertoire will assist in warding off forbidden fruit. In addition to the music that streams from the extension of your soul, emotions are usually stirred.

Dance to lively music. Dancing affords you a method of artistic expression and provides a perfect platform for combining music with emotion. If you are dancing with a partner, the emotion becomes directed and focused - just the ticket to defeat forbidden fruit.

By working to aggressively distract your mind, your thoughts that are consumed with forbidden fruit will begin to wane in strength until you are able to fully disengage them.

Get Vigorous Physical Exercise (if able)

Go To A Gym. Most modern gyms and fitness centers are well equipped with the very latest in exercise equipment and machinery, designed to provide you with a measured workout tailored to your specific needs. From walking, to running, to exercising every muscle group in your body, you can do it all in about thirty minutes per session. Working up a sweat and getting your heart rate up will do wonders for getting your mind off of forbidden fruit.

Play basketball, tennis, or football. These three are representative of very hearty and vigorous activities involving competition and mental toughness. Being fully engaged will force your thoughts to be focused on your activity rather than things that you need to avoid.

Go kayaking. As water activities go, few offer the complete physical workout of kayaking. Focusing on your upper body strength, kayaking will challenge your endurance. A successful kayaking outing will not only provide the break that your mind longs for, but will also immerse you in the beauty of nature with all the attendant sights, sounds, and smells, and that is something your soul will enjoy also.

Go jogging or for a brisk walk. Recognized as one of the most natural exercises and also one that pays the greatest returns for time invested, a brisk walk or light jogging will relieve your mind of its incessant trappings on forbidden fruit. As your body works up a light sweat and your heart rate increases, your mind becomes one with nature as you enjoy your surroundings.

Swim several laps. Swimming is touted as an activity that exercises almost every muscle group. While nothing is over stressed as you glide through the water, your heart rate and respiration increase uniformly and your mind is released from its obsessive patterns.

Go hiking. Hiking a mountain or wooded trail is a proven way to release stress, commune with nature, enjoy the surrounding beauty, and get good exercise all at the same time. If your hike is on a sunny day, you get to enjoy the additional benefit that affords.

Go skiing or ice-skating. Cold weather sports are particularly invigorating owing to the added challenge of the weather. Combine cold air, fresh snow, deep blue cloudless skies, and the stage is set for a beneficial day of skiing or ice skating. Forbidden fruit stands little chance of keeping it's clutches on you in the presence of this activity.

Physical activity is one of nature's best ways of clearing your mind, restoring your spirit, and invigorating you. A word of caution, make sure you are physically able to perform any of the listed activities before engaging in them, and if you are unsure, please see your health care professional.

In summary, allowing forbidden fruit to become food for thought will derail your efforts for a better life with the Law of Attraction. But you do not have to succumb.

You can learn to recognize the familiar symptoms of your mind thinking to excess and entering a downward spiral that gets tighter and faster and stop the process before you crash and burn. This mind block will present your greatest challenge since your ego lives for such situations when it can demonstrate its prowess. You must step in and retake control to restore your thought patterns to those consistent with correctly employing the Law of Attraction. By doing so, you assure yourself that you will attract back into your life what you think about, and your tomorrows will be what you think about today. Your future is in your hands alone!

It's The Law!

Epilogue

I wanted to write this Epilogue to share with you some successes using the Law of Attraction. I have personally used it to manifest a new job that I started just four weeks before starting this book. I also used this law to visualize and attract into my life the condo where I lived while working at that job. My home is in Indiana and the new job was in Michigan so I needed a nice place to live and had a vision of what that looked like and it showed up just at the right time.

From reading the book, you know the current thoughts I have planted concerning the new (to me) boat, my retirement from engineering, and my full engagement in my writing career. Things are progressing well overall, I have finished this book, have several others started, have my personal website set up, and am moving forward at a good pace. I have just recently used this law to semi-retire and work from my home in Indiana as a consulting engineer and a writer.

I have personal knowledge of others who have employed this law in a positive way on purpose for their betterment. One lady has manifested a new job by using this law. She states that at first she thought the Law of Attraction was nonsense, but tried it anyhow. She had a failed attempt where she reports that she had actually focused on what she didn't want and attracted that back into her life. She tried again and visualized herself in a new job at her office and planted thoughts to that affect. Six months later she was promoted to the job she had dreamed of.

Another lady has used the Law of Attraction to create an abundant and prosperous life for herself. She faithfully planted thoughts, thought from the end, had a continual attitude of gratitude and visualized the conditions she wanted to create as already existing. Today she enjoys an abundant lifestyle and has the time to enjoy the things she wants to do.

Another lady uses the Law of Attraction as a philosophy of life. She fixes various images in her mind of what she wants to attract in her life and then thinks as if she already has it and says she can taste, feel, smell, touch and hear it just as she imagines it and then expresses her heartfelt gratitude. As an Associate Professor of Nursing for many years and having obtained her MSN, RN, and CNS credentials, she teaches her students to use visualization as a means to achieve their dream of becoming a registered nurse. She reports that from day one she sets aside time daily for the students to see, hear, taste, smell, and touch the degree and license they will receive in four years.

I personally, have no problem encouraging people to use this law because I know it works just as advertised. If you work the process, recognize the mandates of other universal laws, employ the precepts outlined in this book, you will reap the benefits you desire.

This book was ten weeks in the writing, and reading "The Power of Intention" by Dr. Wayne Dyer and later reading "The Secret" by Rhonda Byrne inspired it. One passage in "The Secret" referenced sowing and reaping and in that split second, I knew I had to write this book because I had a very important contribution to make that no one else had yet made.

I also realized that I had a unique standing in relation to this law. How many other people have as their background twenty-five years as a pastor and over forty years as a mechanical engineer having worked in the field of Quantum Physics on the design team for a particle accelerator? And these two things uniquely come together in explaining the function of the Law of Attraction - who knew?

For years as a pastor I had preached a series of sermons on The Laws of the Harvest that I outlined in skeletal form in Chapter 2 of this book. From what I had read in "The Secret" and heard from a few people I knew that had tried to employ the Law of Attraction, the main question that remained unanswered was "How long will it take before this works for me and I see the results I want?" It was a legitimate question and in that split second, I knew that God had given me the answer years ago, and I therefore had to reveal it. The Law of Attraction behaves in harmony with all of the universal laws of God and the Laws of the Harvest perfectly explain the time delay. I knew that others would benefit from my knowledge of years ago and thus I was compelled to write this book.

I had started writing another book the first of the year but had not been inspired like I was with this book. At the age of sixty-four, I had finally found my true purpose in life and it was writing and public speaking. As I began to write, I found that my experience closely paralleled that of Dr. Wayne Dyer - these were not my words at all. In fact, there were times when I was writing I had to ask the Lord to slow down because I couldn't keep up. As I read back over the chapters, I marveled at what had been written because much of it I had never even thought about much less written down or thought my way through it. Where was this all coming from?

For example, I had never even considered the topic of Chapter 7, The Language of Thought. One day while I was writing, the thought crossed my mind and I began to contemplate adding a small blurb about it somewhere. The small blurb became a full chapter and I have no idea where all of that came from - they are not my words. But I learned a lot about it.

Bibliography

1. Excerpt from: "Wikipedia", "en.wikipedia.org/wiki/Scientific_laws"
2. Excerpt from: "Wikipedia", "en.wikipedia.org/wiki/Laws_of_attraction"
3. Excerpt from: U.S. Andersen, "Three Magic Words", BN Publishing, Kindle Book
4. Excerpt from: Rhonda Byrne, "The Secret", Atria Books/Beyond Words, iBook
5. Excerpt from: Neville Goddard, "The Power Of Awareness", Jazzybee Publishing, iBook
6. Excerpt from: Mark Twain,
7. Excerpt from: "Wikipedia","en.wikipedia.org/wiki/Doubt"
8. Excerpt from: "Fermilab Website, "www.fnal.gov/pub/about/index.html",
9. Excerpt from: "Wikipedia", "en.wikipedia.org/wiki/Gravity
10. Excerpt from: "Wikipedia", "en.wikipedia.org/wiki/Strong_Interaction"
11. Excerpt from: Charles F. Haanel. "The Master Key System." Vigo Books, 2012-04-25. iBook.

Bible verses for the Laws of the Harvest

1st Law - You Reap Only What Has Been Sown - Galatians 6:7

2nd Law - You Reap The Same In Kind As You Sow - Genesis 1: 11-12

3rd Law - You Reap In Proportion as You Sow - 2 Corinthians 9:6

4th Law - You Reap More Than You Sow - Hosea 8:7

5th Law - You Reap In A different Season Than You Sow - Genesis 8:22; Galatians 6:9

www.ingramcontent.com/pod-product-compliance
Lightning Source LLC
Chambersburg PA
CBHW070955040426
42443CB00007B/511